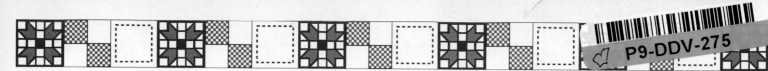

Property of
Mrs. Colvert

Quilt
Math

by Cindi Mitchell

S C H O L A S T I C
PROFESSIONAL BOOKS

New York ○ Toronto ○ London ○ Auckland ○ Sydney

New Delhi ○ Mexico City ○ Hong Kong ○ Buenos Aires

This book is dedicated to the quilters in my family who came before me.

Dorothy H. Neibler, my mother
Margaret Elizabeth Neibler, my paternal grandmother
Flora E. Harmon, my maternal great grandmother
Anna Dorthea Neibler, my paternal great grandmother
Rosa Belle Blades, my paternal great grandmother

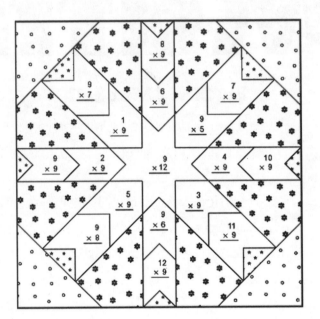

Cindi Mitchell is currently working on a quilt with her mother, Dorothy H. Neibler,
which will be given to her son, Ben Mitchell, upon his graduation from high school.

Scholastic Inc. grants teachers permission to photocopy the activity sheets from this book for classroom use. No other part of this publication may be
reproduced in whole or in part, or stored in a retrieval system, or transmitted in any form or by any means, electronic, mechanical, photocopying,
recording, or otherwise, without written permission of the publisher.
For information regarding permission, write to Scholastic Inc., 557 Broadway, New York, NY 10012-3999.

Cover design by Maria Lilja
Interior design and illustrations by Cindi, Ben, and Jim Mitchell

ISBN: 0-439-37662-9
Copyright © 2003 by Cindi Mitchell
Published by Scholastic Inc.
All rights reserved.
Printed in U.S.A.

1 2 3 4 5 6 7 8 9 10   40   09 08 07 06 05 04 03

Contents

Continued

Continued

Introduction

In my family, I have the awesome responsibility of being the "keeper of the old quilts." I have old quilts hanging on walls, placed over banisters, and tucked away in cupboards. Some quilts are so old and tattered that we have taken pieces of them and preserved them inside picture frames.

Many of the women in my family who came before me have been quilters. Some of them made quilts as a means of income, while others made them to warm their families at night. One of my grandmothers, Margaret Elizabeth Neibler, made crazy quilts out of scraps of satin and velvet, then decorated them with beautiful embroidered flowers.

On a cold winter night I like nothing better than to curl up in my great grandmother's quilt. Like every quilt she made, this one possesses a little part of her—the time she spent choosing the colors and the hours hand-piecing each little square. Now when I breathe in the scent of it, I imagine I can smell her perfume, and as I wrap it around my shoulders, I imagine she is bending over me, giving me a gentle hug.

Quilt Math brings together math, art, and the time-honored tradition of quilting. As students explore the quilt block designs in this book, they will see that what they are learning about shapes, flips, turns, and symmetry in geometry has practical applications in the creative art of quilting. At the same time, they will practice important basic skills in number sense, place value, estimation, addition, subtraction, multiplication, and division. Of course, no quilt activity book would be complete without challenging students to use what they have learned about quilts to design their own quilt blocks.

As your students work on the quilt block activity pages in this book, I hope that they learn to see the art in math and the math in art—and learn to love them both!

How to Use This Book

Each reproducible activity page in this book has four parts:

Math Skill See at a glance the math skill focus of the activity.

Quilt Fact This section includes information about the geometry of each quilt block, the history of quilt making, or specific facts about the quilt block featured on the page. Read this information aloud to students or invite them to read it on their own.

Quilt Block Each quilt block design contains math problems for students to solve. After completing all of the math problems, students color their quilt block using the key near the bottom of the page as a guide. Reading the key gives students practice in following directions and additional practice in math. Students will need a 16-pack of crayons or colored pencils to color their quilt blocks.

Extra! This extension activity reinforces the math skill or relates to the geometry of the quilt block on the page. Invite students to complete this section after they have finished coloring the quilt block. Answers can be found on page 111.

Once students have completed the activity pages, consider making a Collaborative Quilt Art display in your classroom. Simply mount each quilt block on a square of construction paper and place the squares together on a bulletin board.

The last five activities in the book (pages 106–110) give students the opportunity to create their own quilt block designs and apply the geometry concepts they have learned. But don't stop here! Challenge your students further by trying some of the Taking It Further activities below.

Taking It Further

✂ Give each student a handful of pattern blocks and a sheet of 1-inch grid paper. Ask students to create a quilt block on the grid paper using any three pattern blocks.

✂ Give each student one pattern block triangle to trace on a sheet of grid paper. Then challenge students to create a quilt block using only that size triangle. Direct them to center their pattern on the grid. Then tell them that they may flip or turn the triangle to create their design. Afterward, invite them to color and name their quilt block.

✂ Invite each student to design a quilt block on grid paper using three different shapes. One of the shapes must be an octagon.

✂ Encourage each student to design a quilt block that has one line of symmetry, as shown in the quilt blocks at right.

✂ Let students research quilt block patterns in books or on the Internet. Have them reproduce on grid paper one of the patterns they find.

✂ Have students each design and color a 6- by 6-inch quilt block using their favorite shapes and colors. Place them together on a wall to make a class quilt.

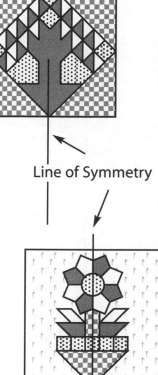

Line of Symmetry

Suggested Resources

Web Site

Women and Geometry: An Archive of American Quilt Patterns
http://womensearlyart.net/quilts/ This web site offers hundreds of American patchwork blocks. Each file includes the name of the block, a photograph of the quilt block created with fabric, and a line drawing of the design.

Books

Quilt-Block History of Pioneer Days, by Mary Cobb (The Millbrook Press, 1995). This delightful book tells the history of the pioneer days through quilts. It includes pictures of dozens of quilt blocks and information about them, as well as projects that kids can make.

Traditional Quilts for Kids to Make, by Barbara J. Eikmeier (The Patchwork Place, 2001). This book includes eight traditional quilt plans and 15 traditional blocks designed especially for children to make. It teaches quiltmaking basics from choosing fabrics to using a sewing machine to rotary cutting and hand-quilting.

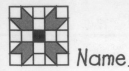

Name_____

Tumbling Blocks

In 1863, Jane Sickle made a large quilt with 225 different quilt block patterns. One of the patterns in the quilt was named Tumbling Blocks.

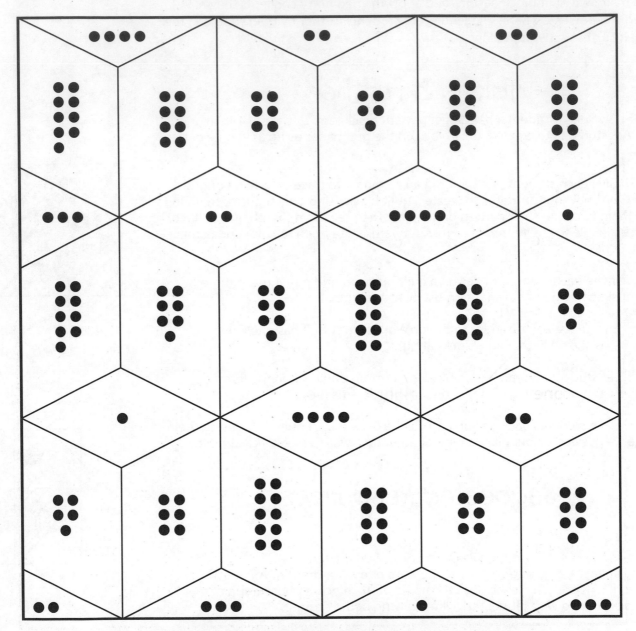

Count the dots.

If the number is	Color the shape
1 or 2	green
3 or 4	yellow
5, 6, or 7	red
8, 9, or 10	blue

 Extra! How old are you? Write the number for your age on the back of this page.

Quilt Math   Scholastic Professional Books

Name_____

Family Album

Album quilts help families remember events in their lives. They often include scraps of wedding dresses, baby bonnets, or pieces of political ribbons.

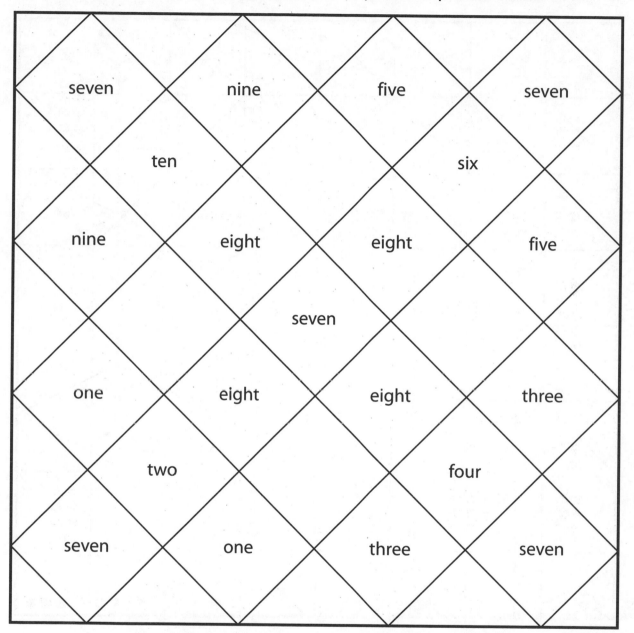

Quilt Math   Scholastic Professional Books

If the number is	Color the shape
1 or 2	green
3 or 4	orange
5 or 6	purple
7 or 8	pink
9 or 10	yellow

Fill in the other shapes with colors of your choice.

Extra! How old are you? Write the word name for your age on the back of this page.

 Name_____

Queen Victoria's Crown

Victoria became the Queen of England in 1837. Many quilt patterns were named in her honor.

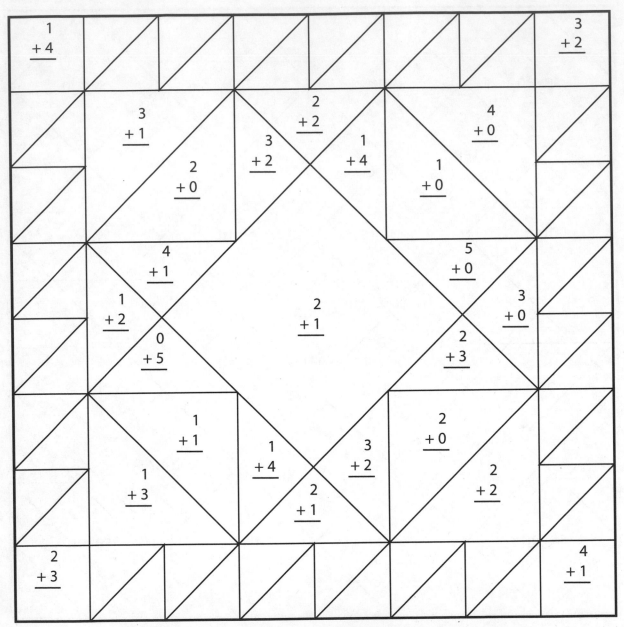

Solve the problems.

If the answer is	Color the shape
1 or 2	red
3 or 4	orange
5	yellow

Fill in the other shapes with colors of your choice.

 Extra! On the back of this page, write an addition problem that has a sum of 5.

10

Quilt Math   Scholastic Professional Books

Name_____

Altar Steps

There are four rectangles inside this quilt block. Can you find them all?

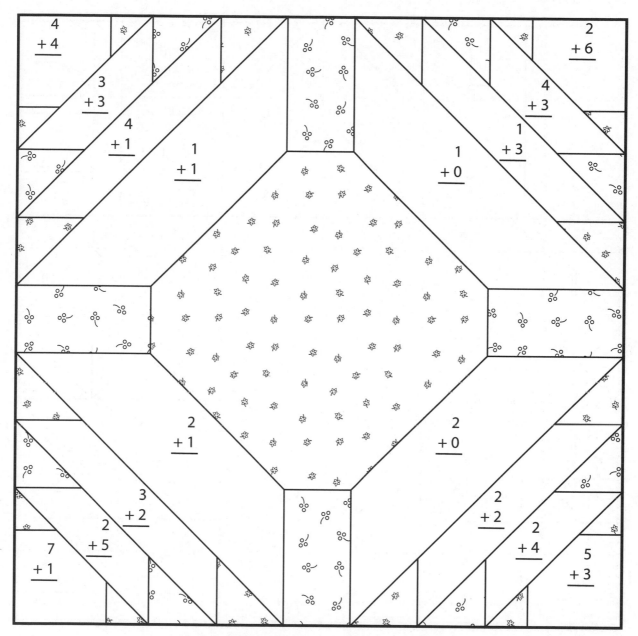

Solve the problems.

If the answer is	Color the shape
1, 2, or 3	purple
4 or 5	red
6 or 7	orange
8	yellow

Fill in the other shapes with colors of your choice.

 Draw a rectangle on the back of the page. Write the number of sides that a rectangle has.

Quilt Math   Scholastic Professional Books

11

Name_____

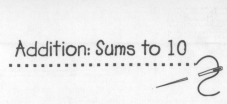

Aunt Ann's Block

This quilt block has 16 squares that are the same size. Can you find them all?

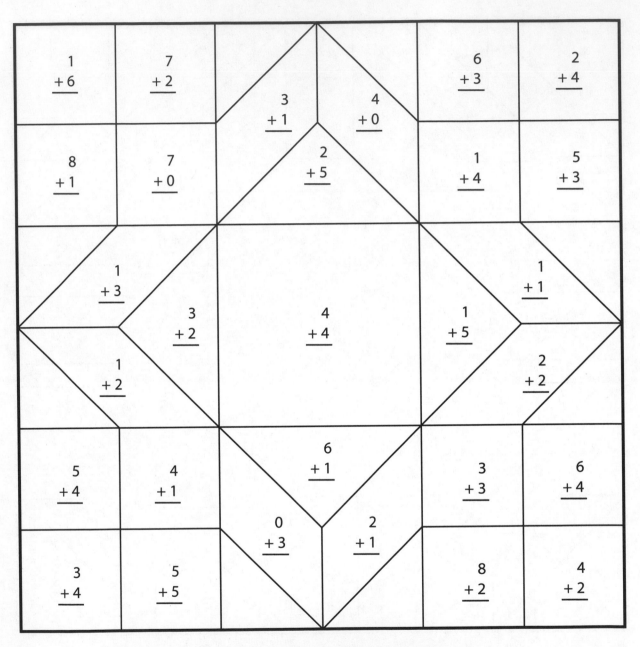

Solve the problems.

If the answer is between	Color the shape
1 and 4	red
5 and 7	blue
8 and 10	yellow

Fill in the other shapes with colors of your choice.

 Extra! Count each side of a square. On the back of this page, write the number of equal-length sides that a square has.

Quilt Math   Scholastic Professional Books

Name_____

Baby Blocks

Baby quilts are often given to parents when a baby is born.

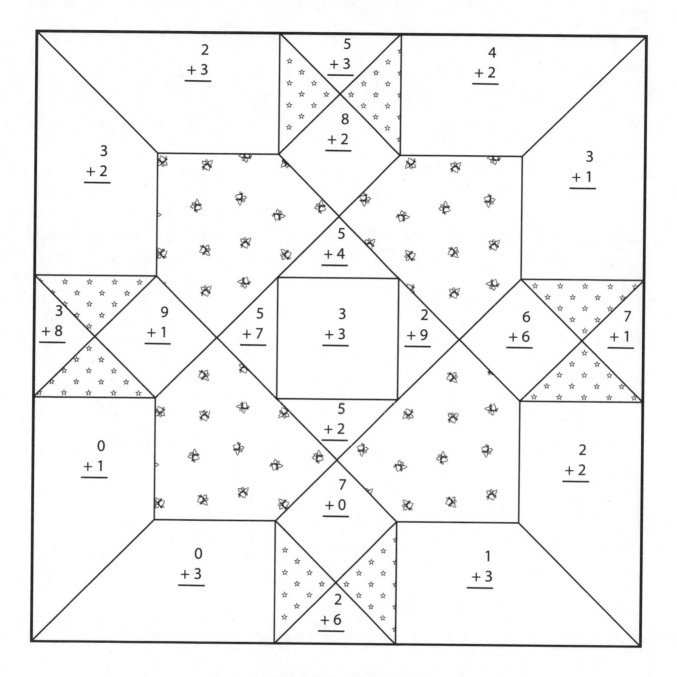

Solve the problems.

If the answer is between	Color the shape
1 and 6	pink
7 and 12	light green

Fill in the other shapes with colors of your choice.

 On the back of this page, write four addition problems that each have an answer of 7.

Quilt Math Scholastic Professional Books

 13

Name_____

Four Pine Trees

This quilt pattern was made over 100 years ago. Can you find the four pine trees?

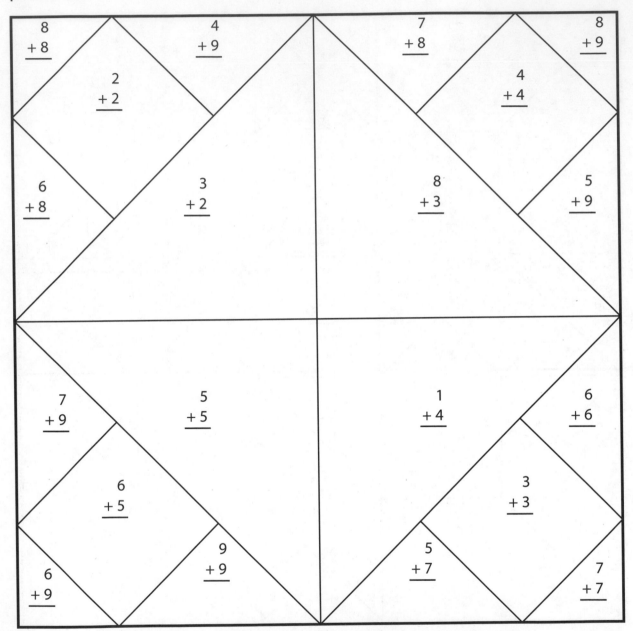

Quilt Math   Scholastic Professional Books

Solve the problems.

If the answer is between	Color the shape
1 and 6	dark green
7 and 11	light green
12 and 18	yellow

 Two shapes were used to make this quilt pattern. Write the names of these shapes on the back of this page.

14

Name_____

Churn Dash

In friendship quilts, each person makes a quilt block and writes his or her name on it. Then the blocks are sewn together to make a quilt.

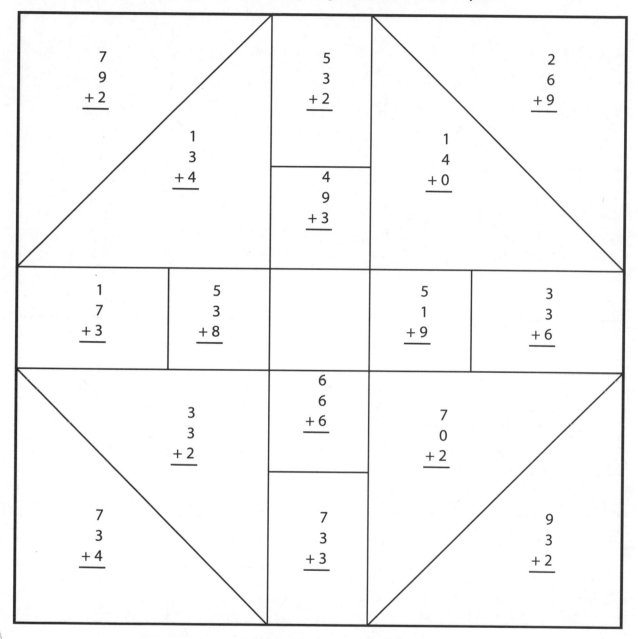

$$\begin{array}{r} 7 \\ 9 \\ +\,2 \\ \hline \end{array}$$

$$\begin{array}{r} 5 \\ 3 \\ +\,2 \\ \hline \end{array}$$

$$\begin{array}{r} 2 \\ 6 \\ +\,9 \\ \hline \end{array}$$

$$\begin{array}{r} 1 \\ 3 \\ +\,4 \\ \hline \end{array}$$

$$\begin{array}{r} 4 \\ 9 \\ +\,3 \\ \hline \end{array}$$

$$\begin{array}{r} 1 \\ 4 \\ +\,0 \\ \hline \end{array}$$

$$\begin{array}{r} 1 \\ 7 \\ +\,3 \\ \hline \end{array}$$

$$\begin{array}{r} 5 \\ 3 \\ +\,8 \\ \hline \end{array}$$

$$\begin{array}{r} 5 \\ 1 \\ +\,9 \\ \hline \end{array}$$

$$\begin{array}{r} 3 \\ 3 \\ +\,6 \\ \hline \end{array}$$

$$\begin{array}{r} 3 \\ 3 \\ +\,2 \\ \hline \end{array}$$

$$\begin{array}{r} 6 \\ 6 \\ +\,6 \\ \hline \end{array}$$

$$\begin{array}{r} 7 \\ 0 \\ +\,2 \\ \hline \end{array}$$

$$\begin{array}{r} 7 \\ 3 \\ +\,4 \\ \hline \end{array}$$

$$\begin{array}{r} 7 \\ 3 \\ +\,3 \\ \hline \end{array}$$

$$\begin{array}{r} 9 \\ 3 \\ +\,2 \\ \hline \end{array}$$

Solve the problems.

If the answer is between	Color the shape
1 and 9	pink
10 and 13	yellow
14 and 18	green

Fill in the other shapes with colors of your choice.

 On the back of this page, write three numbers that when added have a sum of 12.

Quilt Math   Scholastic Professional Books

15

Name_____

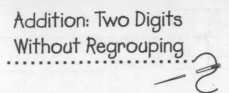

Bow Tie

After coloring, there are four blue bow ties in this quilt block. Can you find them all?

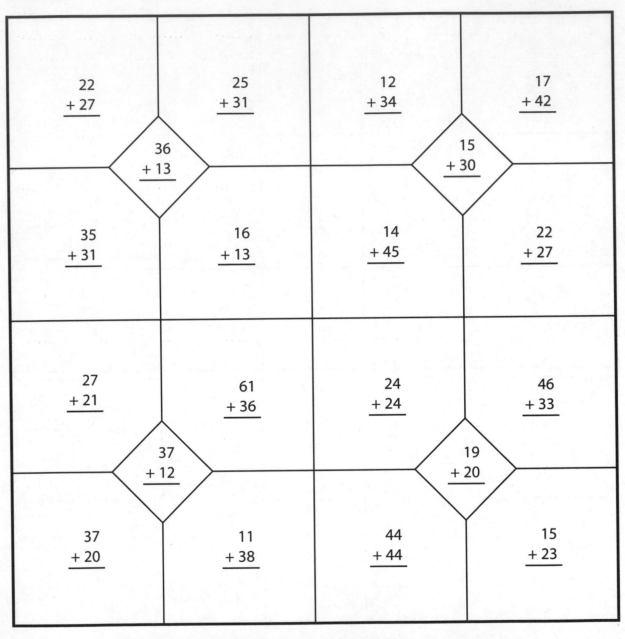

Solve the problems.

If the answer is between	Color the shape
1 and 50	blue
51 and 100	yellow

Extra! What two identical numbers that when added have a sum of 48?
Write the answer on the back of this page.

Quilt Math   Scholastic Professional Books

Name_____

Autumn Leaves

Pioneers often made quilt blocks to look like things they saw every day.
This quilt block looks like a leaf.

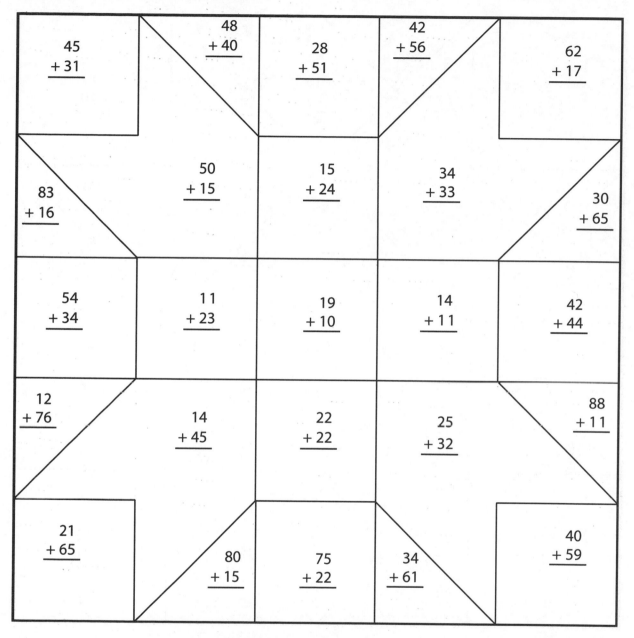

Solve the problems.

If the answer is between	Color the shape
1 and 45	orange
46 and 70	dark orange
71 and 100	green

 On the back of this page, design a quilt block that looks like
something you see every day.

Quilt Math   Scholastic Professional Books

17

Name_____

Lighthouse Beacon

There are four rectangles in this design. Can you find them all?

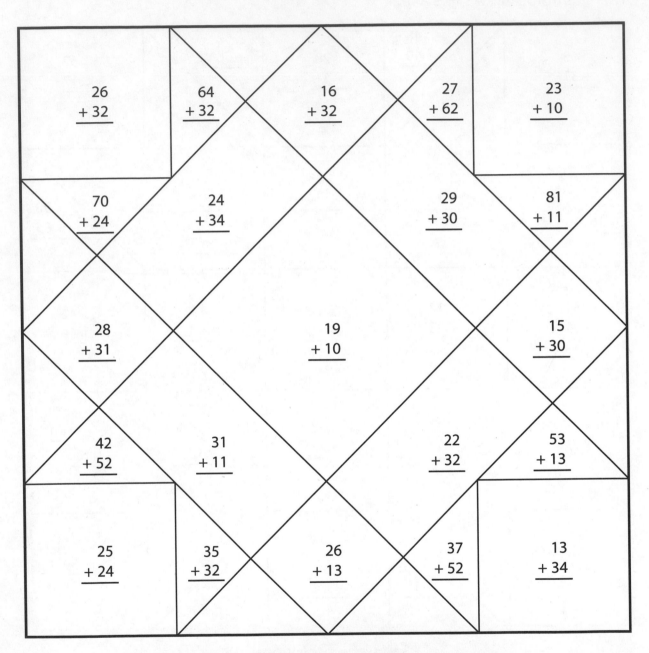

Solve the problems.

If the answer is between	Color the shape
0 and 30	orange
31 and 60	yellow
61 and 99	blue

Fill in the other shapes with colors of your choice.

Quilt Math   Scholastic Professional Books

 Extra! On the back of this page, draw two rectangles that are not the same size.

18

Name_____

Kaleidoscope Patchwork

This quilt block has 20 triangles. Can you find them all?

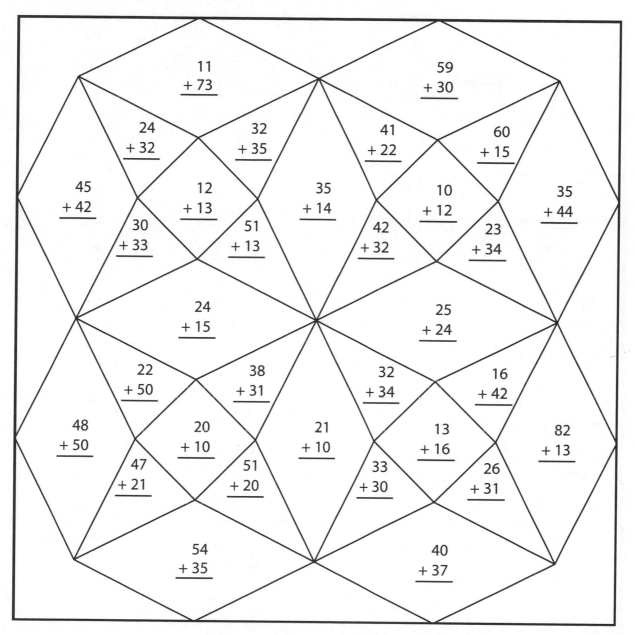

Quilt Math   Scholastic Professional Books

Solve the problems.

If the answer is between	Color the shape
0 and 30	black
31 and 50	pink
51 and 75	purple
76 and 100	yellow

Fill in the other shapes with colors of your choice.

Extra! On the back of this page, draw two triangles that are not the same size.

19

Name_____

Cut the Corners

Quilts are often made for special occasions. Some people make quilts when babies are born or when a couple is married.

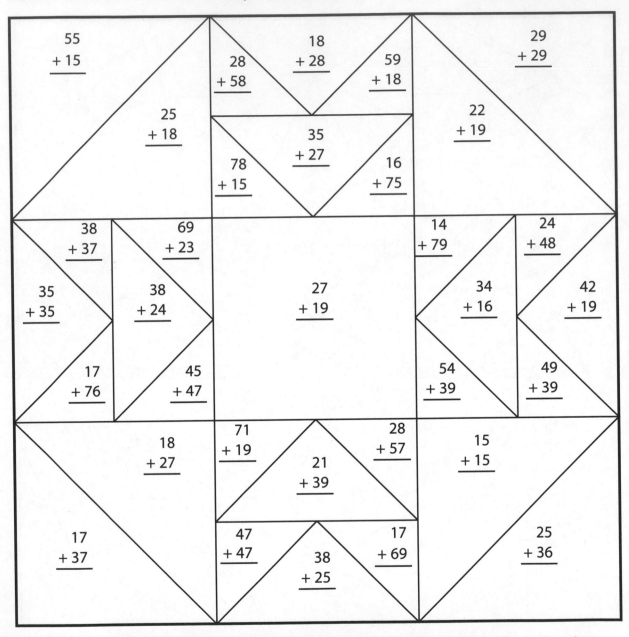

Solve the problems. Then on each line below, write the name of a color that you like. Color the quilt block.

If the answer is between	Color the shape
1 and 45	_____
46 and 70	_____
71 and 100	_____

 Extra! On the back of this page, write an addition problem that has a sum of 99.

20

Quilt Math   Scholastic Professional Books

Name_____

Broken Dishes

In pioneer days, when this quilt block was first made, people did not have plastic dishes. Dishes were very easy to break.

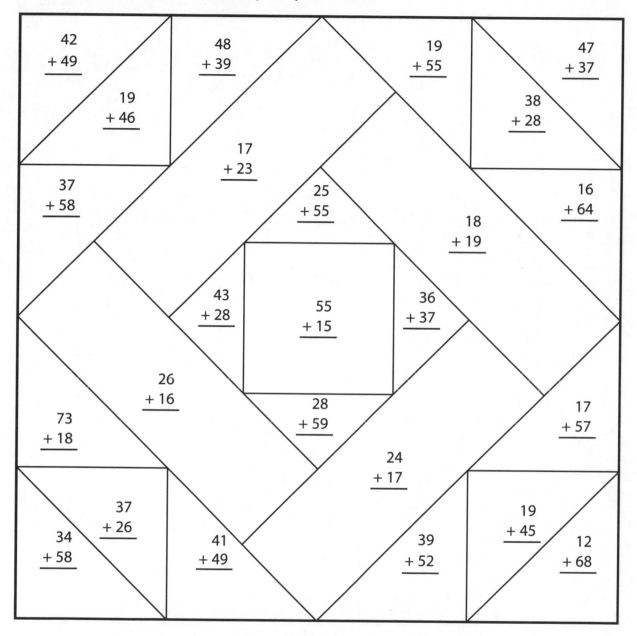

Solve the problems.

If the answer is between	Color the shape
1 and 45	black
46 and 70	pink
71 and 100	purple

 Extra! Fill in the missing digit. $14 + 5\square = 70$

Name _____

Octagon Puzzle

Octagon This shape is an octagon. There are five octagons in this quilt pattern. Can you find them all?

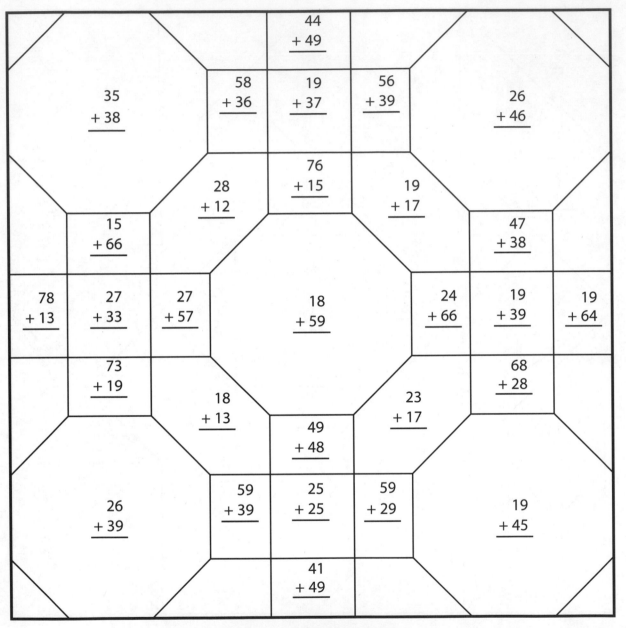

Solve the problems.

If the answer is between	Color the shape
0 and 40	green
41 and 60	yellow
61 and 80	light blue
81 and 99	orange

Fill in the other shapes with colors of your choice.

Extra! Count each side of an octagon. On the back of this page, write the number of sides that you counted.

Quilt Math Scholastic Professional Books

Name_____

Twirling Stars

This quilt block has 24 triangles. Can you find them all?

58
+ 29

44
+ 26

18
+ 28

29
+ 16

14
+ 36

26
+ 36

18
+ 47

27
+ 26

17
+ 18

22
+ 19

15
+ 25

17
+ 27

55
+ 36

32
+ 39

58
+ 36

24
+ 26

24
+ 19

11
+ 19

47
+ 39

28
+ 24

Solve the problems.

If the answer is between	Color the shape
1 and 50	yellow
51 and 99	purple

Fill in the other shapes with colors of your choice.

Quilt Math Scholastic Professional Books

 On the back of this page, write a two-digit addition problem using two odd numbers.

23

Column Addition: Two
Digits With Regrouping

Framed Nine Patch

In pioneer days, eight- and nine-year-old children were taught to make quilt blocks. The Framed Nine Patch was often the first block they learned to make.

17 10 + 14	22 19 + 21	11 27 + 4
27 30 + 13	36 20 7 33 19 31 +14 + 7 +34	5 36 + 24
	19 14 5 11 51 28 +19 +25 +17	
	36 13 20 26 7 53 +21 +25 +27	
14 9 + 10	17 31 + 14	9 9 + 31

Solve the problems.

If the answer is between	Color the shape
1 and 50	green
51 and 70	orange
71 and 100	yellow

 Extra! On the back of this page, write an addition problem with three addends that has a sum of 99.

Quilt Math Scholastic Professional Books

Name_____

Flyfoot

A finished quilt has three layers—the quilt top, batting, and back. These layers are sewn together with little stitches that often make pretty designs.

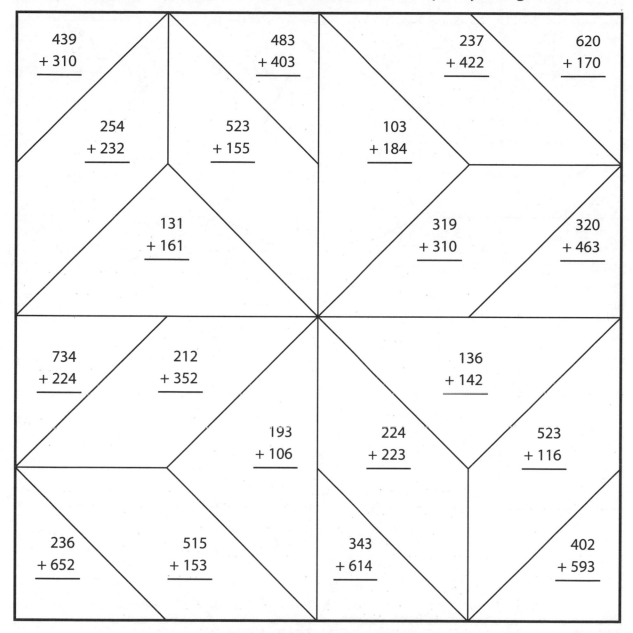

439 + 310	483 + 403	237 + 422	620 + 170
254 + 232	523 + 155	103 + 184	
131 + 161		319 + 310	320 + 463
734 + 224	212 + 352	136 + 142	
	193 + 106	224 + 223	523 + 116
236 + 652	515 + 153	343 + 614	402 + 593

Solve the problems.

If the answer is between	Color the shape
1 and 300	yellow
301 and 700	orange
701 and 1000	green

 Put the digits 8, 1, and 6 in order to make the smallest number possible.

Quilt Math   Scholastic Professional Books

Name_____

Star of the Sea

Pioneer women had quilting bees. Women from the same area met at one house, gathered around a quilting frame, and sewed a quilt together.

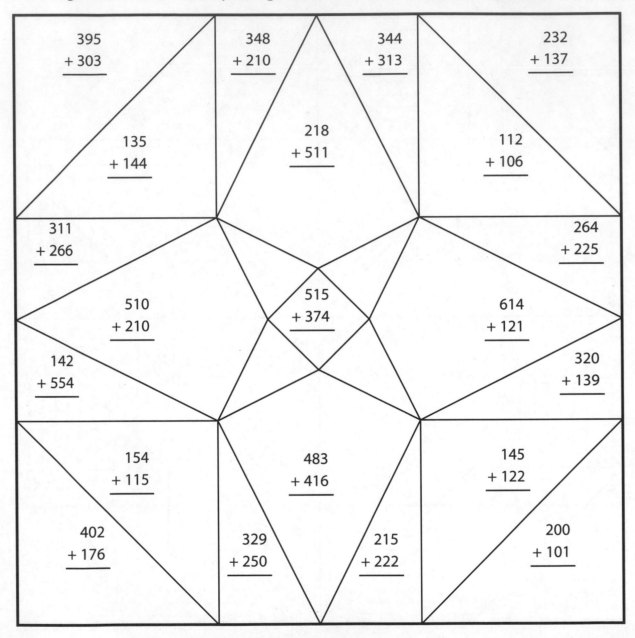

395
+ 303

348
+ 210

344
+ 313

232
+ 137

135
+ 144

218
+ 511

112
+ 106

311
+ 266

264
+ 225

510
+ 210

515
+ 374

614
+ 121

142
+ 554

320
+ 139

154
+ 115

483
+ 416

145
+ 122

402
+ 176

329
+ 250

215
+ 222

200
+ 101

Solve the problems.

If the answer is between	Color the shape
1 and 300	blue
301 and 700	green
701 and 1000	yellow

Fill in the other shapes with colors of your choice.

Extra! What number when added to 302 has the sum of 738? Write your answer on the back of this page.

Quilt Math   Scholastic Professional Books

Name_____

Bright Star

In 1920 quilting became so popular that quilt patterns were published in newspapers and magazines.

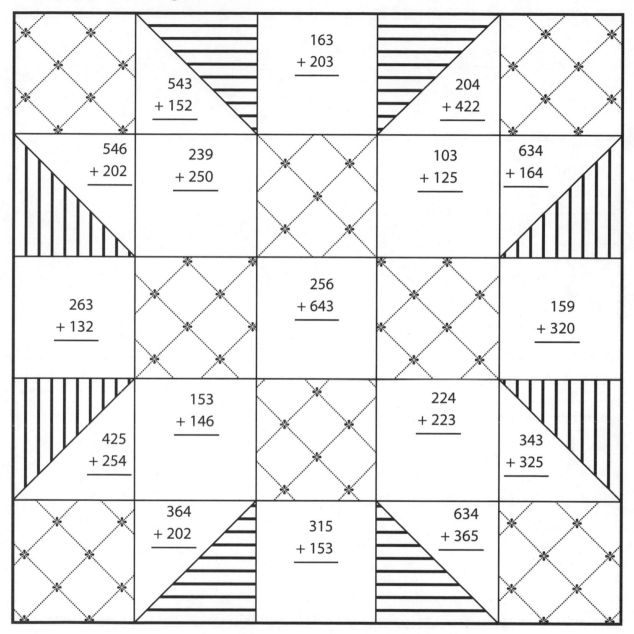

Solve the problems.

If the answer is between	Color the shape
1 and 499	light blue
500 and 999	green

Fill in the other shapes with colors of your choice.

 On the back of this page, write a two-digit addition problem using two even numbers.

Quilt Math   Scholastic Professional Books

27

Name_____

Basket

In pioneer days, people didn't have plastic or paper bags. Baskets were used to carry things. Can you find the basket in this quilt pattern?

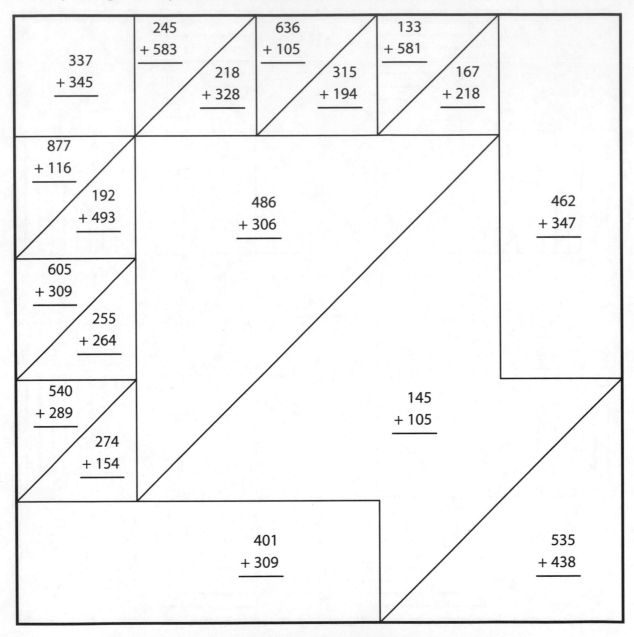

337
+ 345
___

245
+ 583
___

218
+ 328
___

636
+ 105
___

315
+ 194
___

133
+ 581
___

167
+ 218
___

877
+ 116
___

192
+ 493
___

486
+ 306
___

462
+ 347
___

605
+ 309
___

255
+ 264
___

540
+ 289
___

274
+ 154
___

145
+ 105
___

401
+ 309
___

535
+ 438
___

Quilt Math Scholastic Professional Books

Solve the problems.

If the answer is between	Color the shape
1 and 300	yellow
301 and 700	green
701 and 1000	blue

Put the digits 1, 5, and 7 in order to make the largest number possible. Then, put these same digits in order to make the smallest number possible. Find the sum of the two numbers.

Name_____

Addition: Three Digits With Regrouping

Biloxi

On the Oregon Trail, people used quilts for many things. They were placed on wagon seats as cushions and hung on the sides of wagons to block the sun.

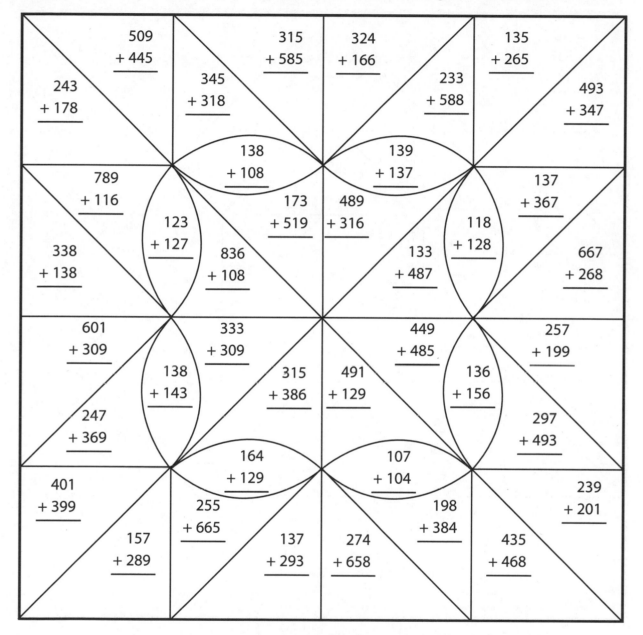

Solve the problems.

If the answer is between	Color the shape
1 and 300	yellow
301 and 500	red
501 and 700	blue
701 and 1000	green

 Write three addition problems that each have a sum between 1 and 300.

Quilt Math Scholastic Professional Books

29

Name_____

Pinwheel

In colonial times, girls made 12 quilts to take with them when they married.
Their thirteenth quilt, the bridal quilt, was made after a couple was engaged.

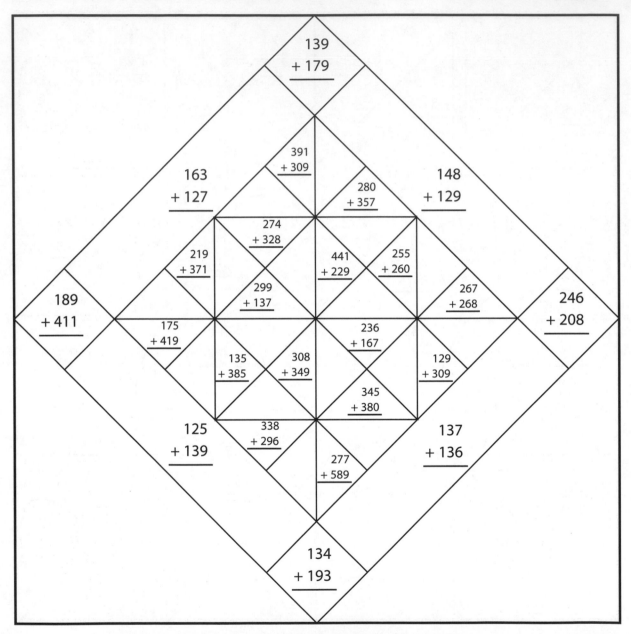

139
+ 179

391
+ 309

163
+ 127

280
+ 357

148
+ 129

274
+ 328

219
+ 371

441
+ 229

255
+ 260

299
+ 137

267
+ 268

189
+ 411

175
+ 419

236
+ 167

246
+ 208

135
+ 385

308
+ 349

129
+ 309

345
+ 380

125
+ 139

338
+ 296

137
+ 136

277
+ 589

134
+ 193

Quilt Math   Scholastic Professional Books

Solve the problems.

If the answer is between	Color the shape
1 and 300	yellow
301 and 600	light green
601 and 999	pink

Fill in the other
shapes with
colors of your
choice.

 Write three digits between 0 and 9, in order, from greatest to least. Then,
rewrite them, in order, from least to greatest. Find the sum of the numbers.

30

Name_____

Rock-a-Bye

This quilt block pattern was designed for a baby quilt.

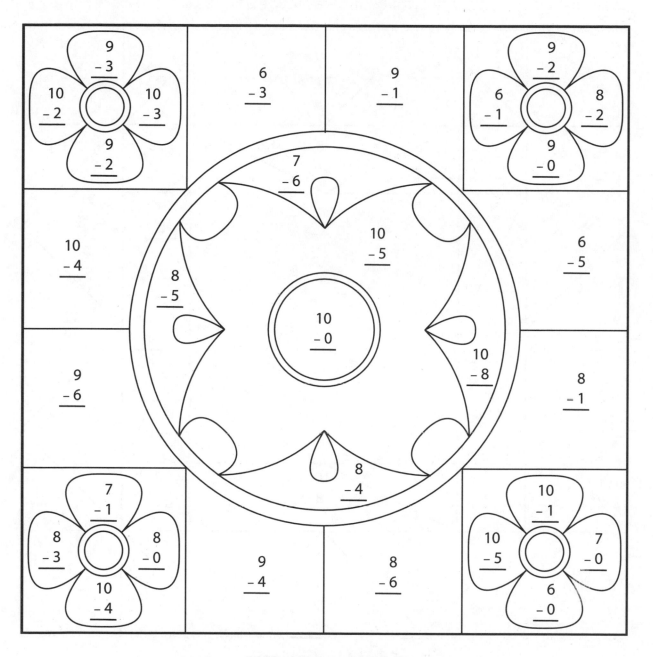

Solve the problems.

If the answer is	Color the shape
1, 2, 3, or 4	blue
5, 6, 7, 8, or 9	pink
10	yellow

Fill in the other shapes with colors of your choice.

Quilt Math   Scholastic Professional Books

 Extra! On the back of this page, write three subtraction problems that each have a difference of 2.

31

Name_____

Evening Star

Star shapes were the patterns used most often in pioneer quilts.

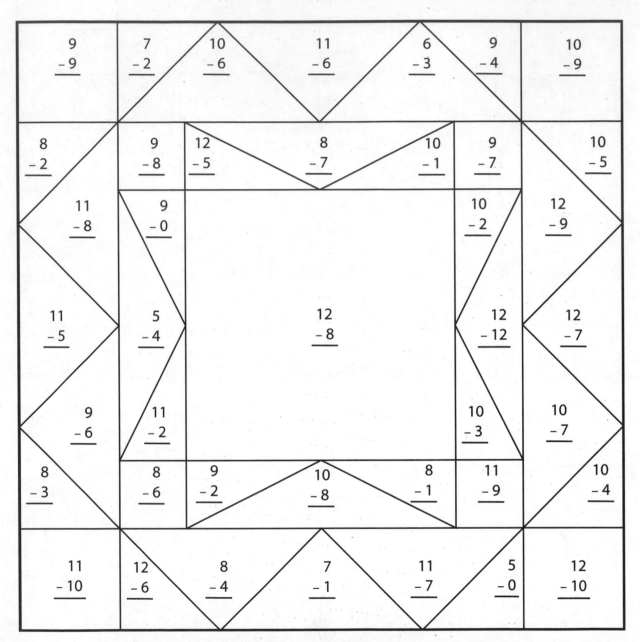

9 −9	7 −2	10 −6	11 −6	6 −3	9 −4	10 −9
8 −2	9 −8	12 −5	8 −7	10 −1	9 −7	10 −5
11 −8	9 −0			10 −2	12 −9
11 −5	5 −4	12 −8		12 −12	12 −7
9 −6	11 −2		10 −3	10 −7
8 −3	8 −6	9 −2	10 −8	8 −1	11 −9	10 −4
11 −10	12 −6	8 −4	7 −1	11 −7	5 −0	12 −10

Quilt Math   Scholastic Professional Books

Solve the problems.

If the answer is	Color the shape
0, 1, or 2	brown
3 or 4	orange
5 or 6	black
7, 8, 9, or 10	yellow

 Extra! On the back of this page, write three subtraction problems that each have a difference of 4.

Name_____

Sunburst

It takes an expert quilter to make a sunburst pattern because it is hard to sew all of the little points together in the center.

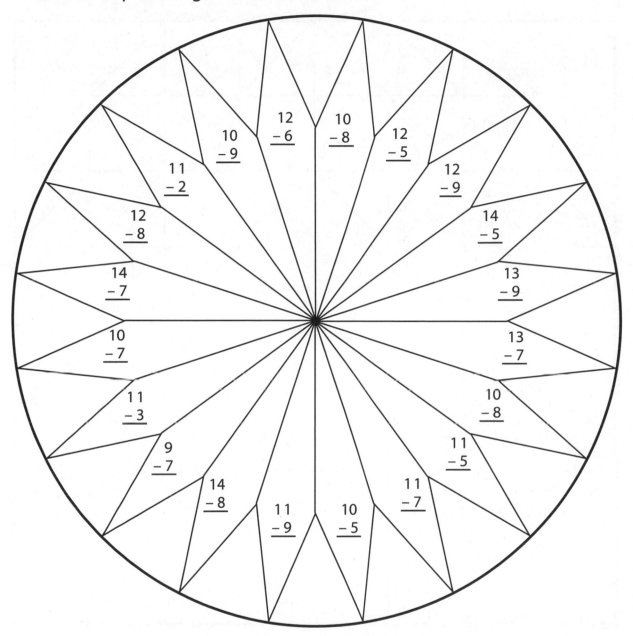

Solve the problems.

If the answer is between	Color the shape
1 and 4	orange
5 and 9	yellow

Fill in the other shapes with colors of your choice.

 Extra! On the back of this page, write the word names in order for the numbers 10 through 14.

Quilt Math Scholastic Professional Books

33

Name_____

Ocean Wave

Many quilt patterns were named for things in nature. Why do you think this pattern is called Ocean Wave?

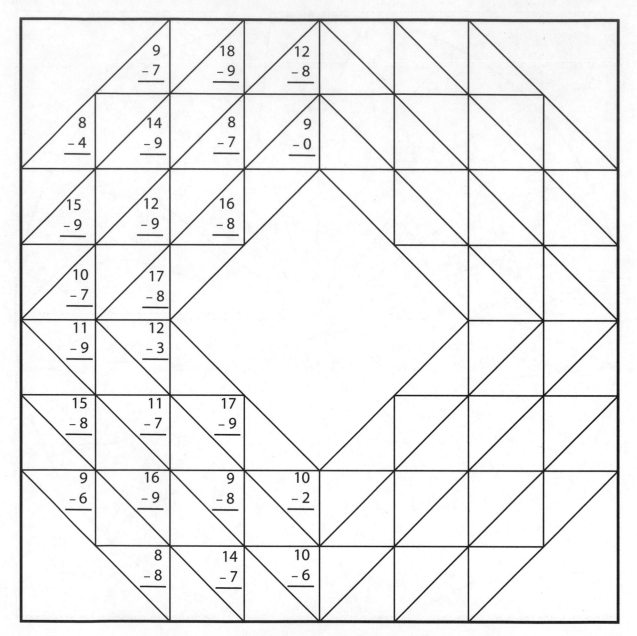

Solve the problems.

If the answer is between	Color the shape
0 and 4	green
5 and 9	blue

 Color the other half of the design so that both sides match. Then fill in the other shapes with colors of your choice.

Quilt Math   Scholastic Professional Books

Name_____

Flying Geese

There are two different sizes of triangles in this quilt block. Can you find them both?

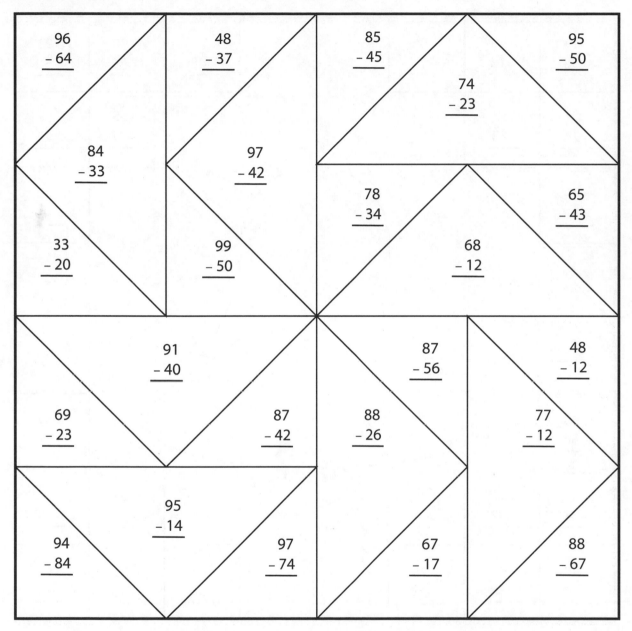

Solve the problems.

If the answer is between	Color the shape
1 and 50	brown
51 and 99	green

 On the back of this page, write two subtraction problems that each have the same difference.

Quilt Math   Scholastic Professional Books

35

Name_____

Cow Bell

Why did pioneers put bells on their cows? Cows wandered away as they ate grass. When the bells rang, the cow owners knew where to look for the cows!

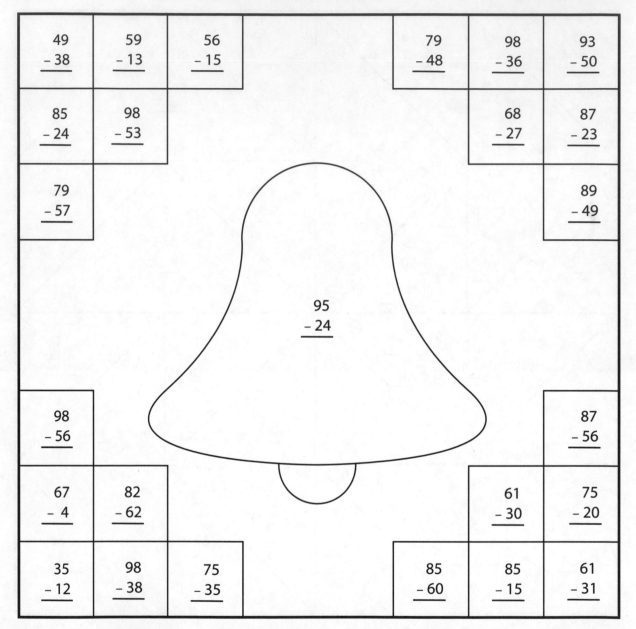

49 – 38	59 – 13	56 – 15	79 – 48	98 – 36	93 – 50
85 – 24	98 – 53			68 – 27	87 – 23
79 – 57					89 – 49

95
– 24

98 – 56					87 – 56
67 – 4	82 – 62			61 – 30	75 – 20
35 – 12	98 – 38	75 – 35	85 – 60	85 – 15	61 – 31

Solve the problems.

If the answer is between	Color the shape
1 and 45	red
46 and 70	blue
71 and 100	yellow

Fill in the other shapes with colors of your choice.

 On the back of this page, write the word name for a number between 40 and 50.

Quilt Math   Scholastic Professional Books

Name_____

Sky Rocket

In colonial days, males helped make quilts. Boys helped cut fabric and sew.
Some men even designed the wedding quilt made by their bride.

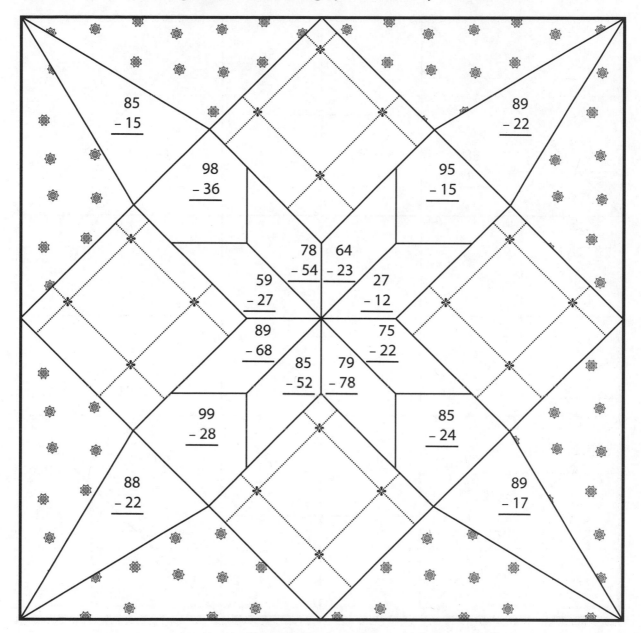

Solve the problems.

If the answer is between	Color the shape
1 and 30	light orange
31 and 60	dark orange
61 and 99	green

Fill in the other
shapes with
colors of your
choice.

 On the back of this page, write a two-digit subtraction problem using
only numbers between 0 and 5.

Quilt Math   Scholastic Professional Books

37

Name_____

Prairie Queen

In this quilt pattern, there are 16 squares that are the same size. Can you find them all?

$$96 - 12$$

$$98 - 56$$ $$79 - 55$$ $$78 - 22$$

$$97 - 16$$ $$88 - 67$$

$$58 - 45$$ $$85 - 22$$ $$87 - 15$$

$$89 - 58$$ $$95 - 72$$ $$60 - 20$$

$$99 - 35$$

Quilt Math   Scholastic Professional Books

Solve the problems.

If the answer is between	Color the shape
1 and 30	dark green
31 and 60	light green
61 and 99	brown

Fill in the other shapes with colors of your choice.

Extra! On the back of this page, write a two-digit subtraction problem using only odd numbers.

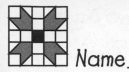

Name_____

Army Star

Eight-pointed stars were worn on Army uniforms in the Civil War. Can you find the star in this quilt block?

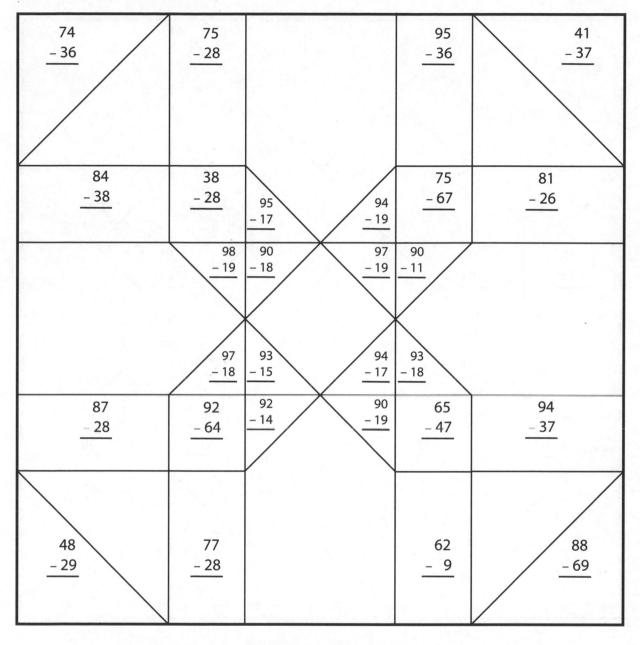

Solve the problems.

If the answer is between	Color the shape
1 and 45	red
46 and 70	blue
71 and 99	yellow

Fill in the other shapes with colors of your choice.

Extra! Write a subtraction problem that has an answer greater than 80.

Quilt Math   Scholastic Professional Books

39

Name_____

Northumberland Star

There are three different sizes of triangles in this quilt block. Can you find them all?

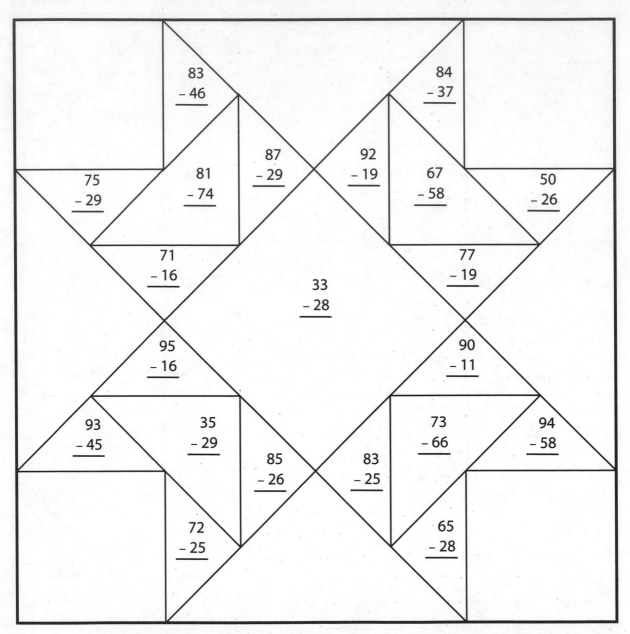

83
− 46

84
− 37

87
− 29

92
− 19

75
− 29

81
− 74

67
− 58

50
− 26

71
− 16

77
− 19

33
− 28

95
− 16

90
− 11

93
− 45

35
− 29

73
− 66

94
− 58

85
− 26

83
− 25

72
− 25

65
− 28

Solve the problems.

If the answer is between	Color the shape
1 and 10	yellow
11 and 50	blue
51 and 99	green

Fill in the other shapes with colors of your choice.

 On the back of this page, use two of these numbers to write a subtraction problem with the largest difference possible: 18, 93, 28, 64.

Quilt Math   Scholastic Professional Books

Name_____

Subtraction: Two Digits
With Regrouping

Barbara Frietchie Star

Barbara Frietchie was a brave woman. She defended the right to fly the
American flag when the Confederate Army marched through her town.

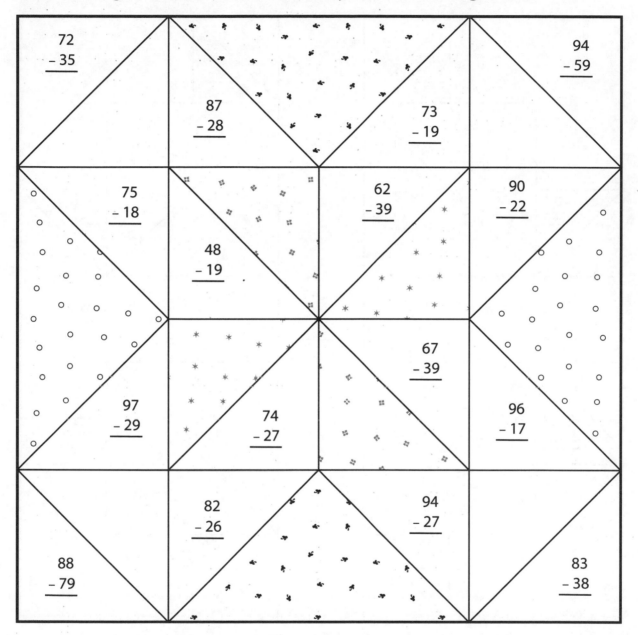

Quilt Math   Scholastic Professional Books

Solve the problems.

If the answer is between	Color the shape
1 and 50	red
51 and 99	blue

Fill in the other
shapes with
colors of your
choice.

 Extra! On the back of this page, write as many subtraction problems as
possible using these numbers: 86, 32, 19, 94.

41

Name_____

Cross and Crown

There is one cross and four crowns in this quilt block. Can you find them all?

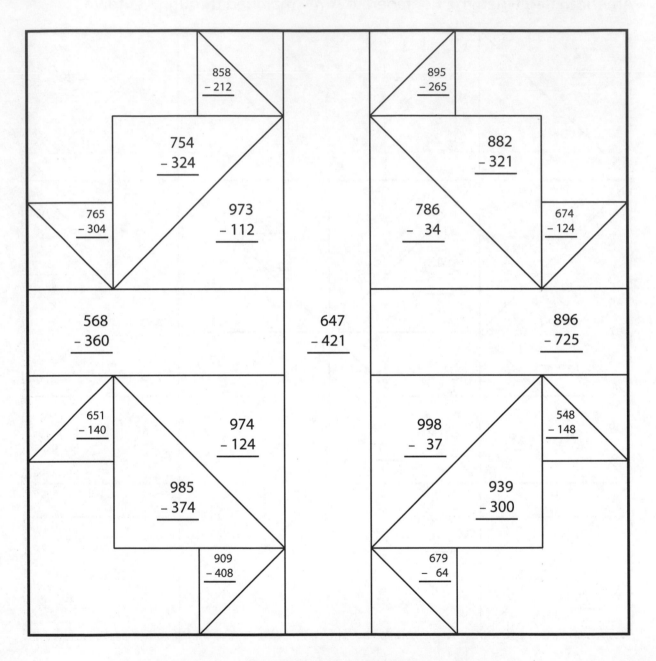

858
− 212

895
− 265

754
− 324

882
− 321

765
− 304

973
− 112

786
− 34

674
− 124

568
− 360

647
− 421

896
− 725

651
− 140

974
− 124

998
− 37

548
− 148

985
− 374

939
− 300

909
− 408

679
− 64

Solve the problems.

If the answer is between	Color the shape
1 and 300	purple
301 and 700	yellow
701 and 1000	black

Fill in the other shapes with colors of your choice.

Quilt Math Scholastic Professional Books

 Extra! This mystery number has four digits and is even. When you subtract it from 877, the difference is 535. Write the mystery number on the back of this page.

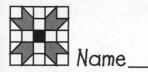

Name_____

Meadow Flower

There are 20 squares in this quilt block that are the same shape and size.
Can you find them all?

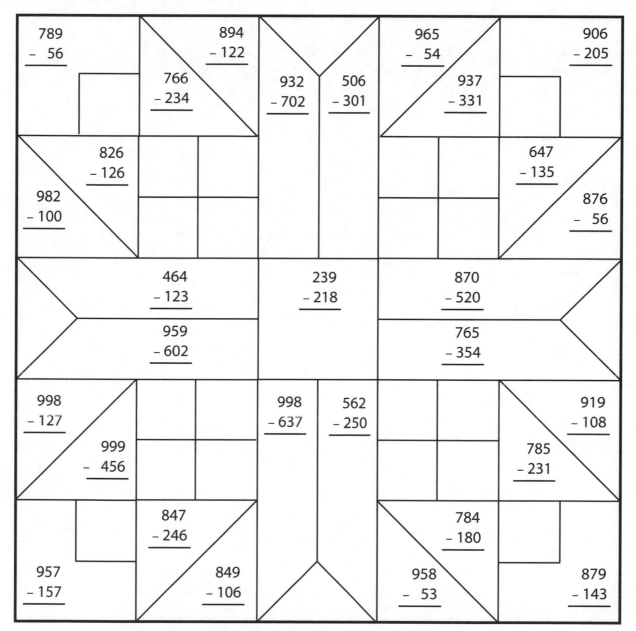

Solve the problems.

If the answer is between	Color the shape
0 and 200	blue
201 and 500	yellow
501 and 700	purple
701 and 1000	orange

Fill in the other
shapes with
colors of your
choice.

Extra! On the back of this page, draw a triangle. Then, draw another triangle
that is the same shape, but bigger.

Quilt Math Scholastic Professional Books

43

Name_____

Falling Star

This quilt block was named after a falling star. It looks like it is falling down, down, down.

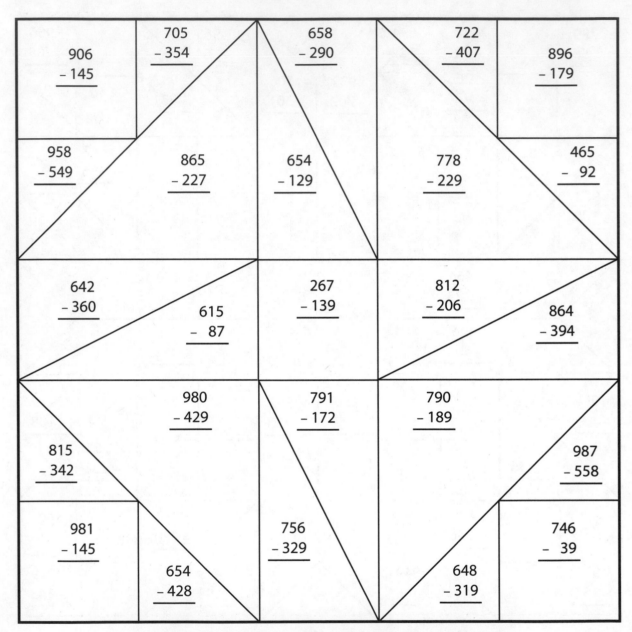

906
– 145

705
– 354

658
– 290

722
– 407

896
– 179

958
– 549

865
– 227

654
– 129

778
– 229

465
– 92

642
– 360

615
– 87

267
– 139

812
– 206

864
– 394

980
– 429

791
– 172

790
– 189

815
– 342

987
– 558

981
– 145

654
– 428

756
– 329

648
– 319

746
– 39

Solve the problems.

If the answer is between	Color the shape
0 and 200	red
201 and 500	blue
501 and 700	dark orange
701 and 1000	yellow

 Extra! On the back of this page, write a subtraction problem that has a difference of 312.

44

Quilt Math   Scholastic Professional Books

Name_____

Eight-Pointed Stars

This quilt block has four rectangles that are the same size and same shape.
Can you find them all?

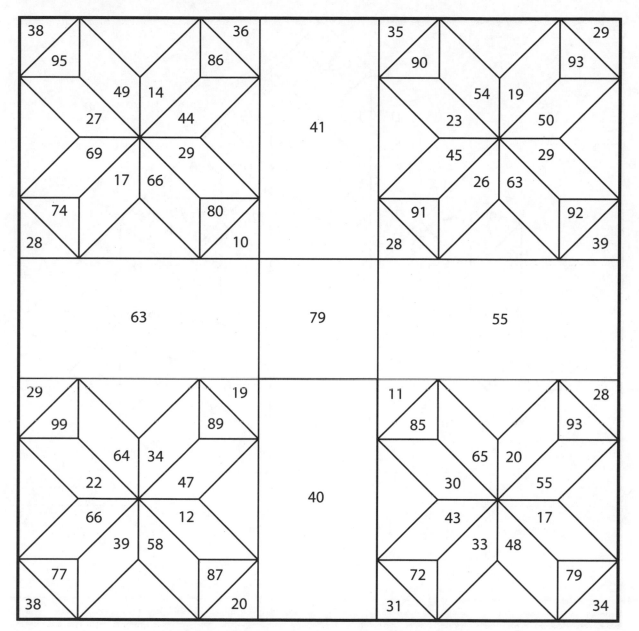

Look at the digits in the tens place.

If the digit is	Color the shape
1, 2, or 3	green
4, 5, or 6	blue
7, 8, or 9	yellow

Fill in the other shapes with colors of your choice.

Quilt Math Scholastic Professional Books

 Count each side of a rectangle. On the back of this page, write the word for the number of sides that a rectangle has.

45

Name_____

Pine Tree

In this quilt block, one half of the tree is a mirror image of the other side.

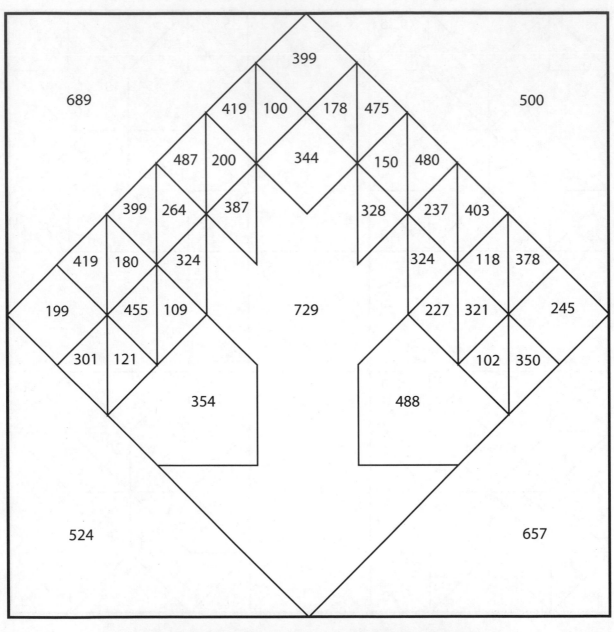

Look at the digits in the hundreds place.

If the digit is	Color the shape
1 or 2	green
3 or 4	blue
5 or 6	yellow
7, 8, or 9	brown

Extra! • Which of these pairs of shapes show a mirror image? Circle them.

Quilt Math   Scholastic Professional Books

Name_____

Vermont Block

This quilt block has many different types and sizes of triangles. Can you find three different sizes of triangles?

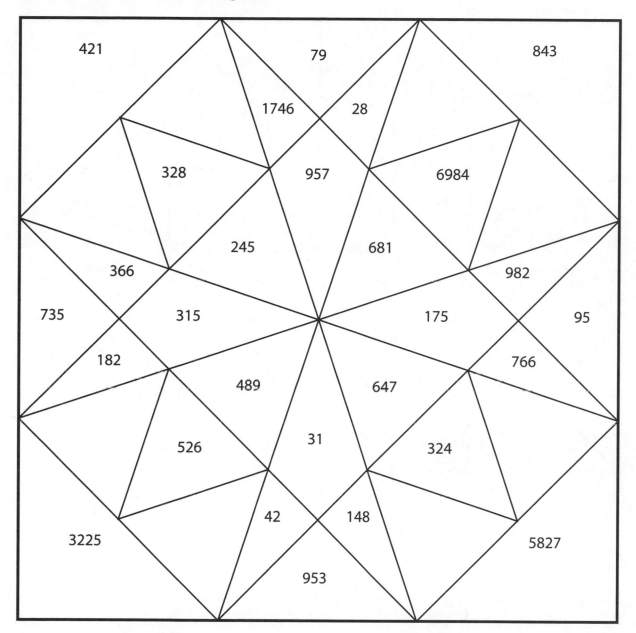

Within the quilt block:
421, 79, 843, 1746, 28, 328, 957, 6984, 245, 681, 366, 982, 735, 315, 175, 95, 182, 766, 489, 647, 526, 31, 324, 42, 148, 3225, 953, 5827

If the number in the	Color the shape
hundreds place is even	blue
tens place is odd	yellow
ones place is even	pink

Fill in the other shapes with colors of your choice.

Extra! On the back of this page, write the largest 3-digit number possible that has all different and odd digits.

Name_____

Broken Star

In this quilt block, there are eight small squares inside one large square.
Can you find all nine squares?

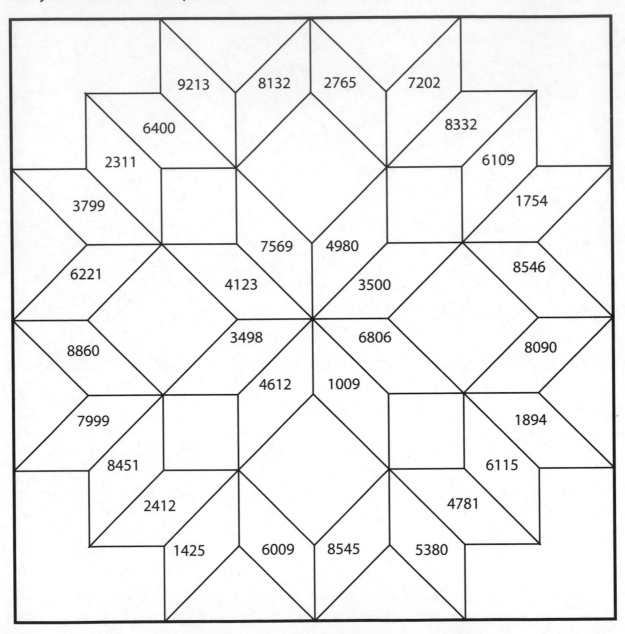

9213 8132 2765 7202
6400 8332
2311 6109
3799 1754
7569 4980
6221 8546
4123 3500
3498 6806
8860 8090
4612 1009
7999 1894
8451 6115
2412 4781
1425 6009 8545 5380

Quilt Math Scholastic Professional Books

On each line below, write the name of a color that you like. Then color the
quilt block.

If the number is	Color the shape
even	_____
odd	_____

Fill in the other
shapes with
colors of your
choice.

Extra! On the back of this page, write the largest 4-digit number possible
that has a 7 in the thousands place.

Name_____

Rising Sun

In colonial days, most women had sewing kits that contained scissors, thread, and needles. They took these kits with them when they went to quilting bees.

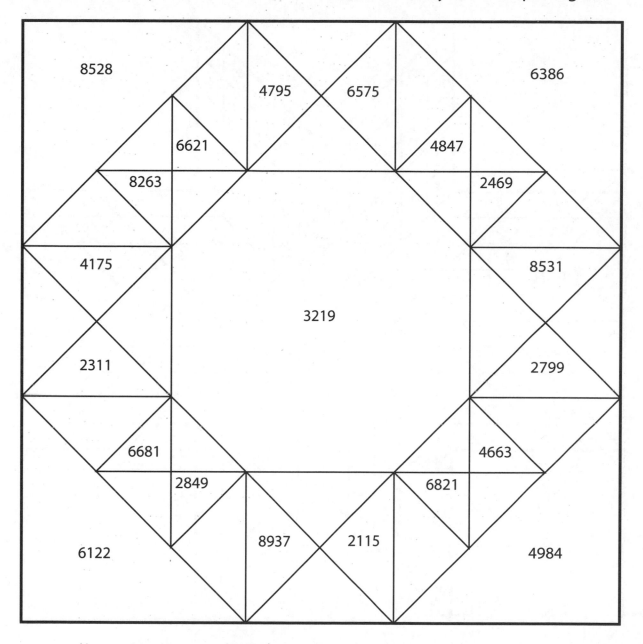

If the number in the	Color the shape
thousands place is odd	purple
hundreds place is even	dark blue
tens place is odd	yellow
ones place is even	dark pink

Fill in the other shapes with colors of your choice.

Extra! On the back of this page, write the largest four-digit number possible that has all different and odd digits.

Quilt Math   Scholastic Professional Books

49

Name_____

Native American Star

This quilt block design was often made by Plains Indian women in the late 1800s.

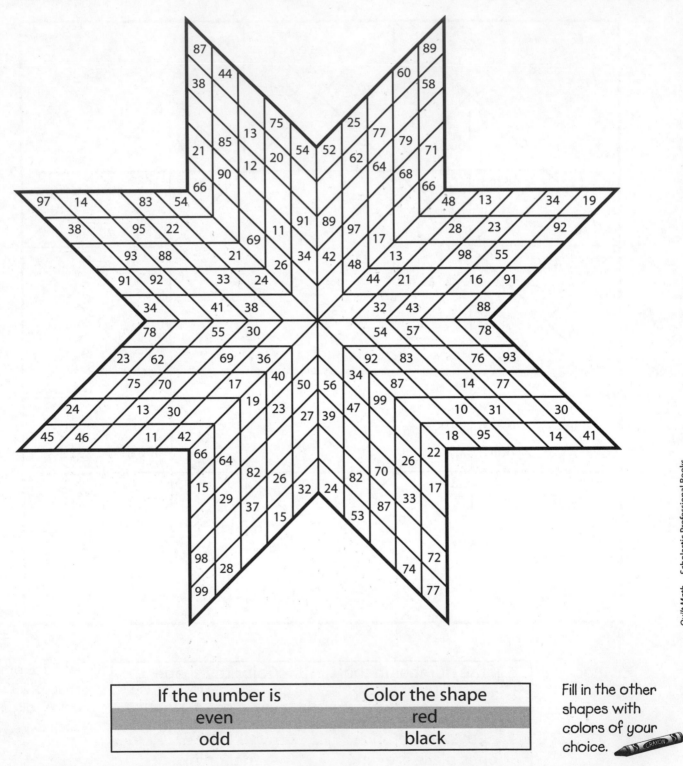

If the number is	Color the shape
even	red
odd	black

Fill in the other shapes with colors of your choice.

Quilt Math   Scholastic Professional Books

 On the back of this page, write an even 3-digit number and an odd 3-digit number. Add the numbers. Is the sum odd or even?

Birds and Stars

This star is made from many triangles that are all the same size. Can you create another shape or design using only triangles?

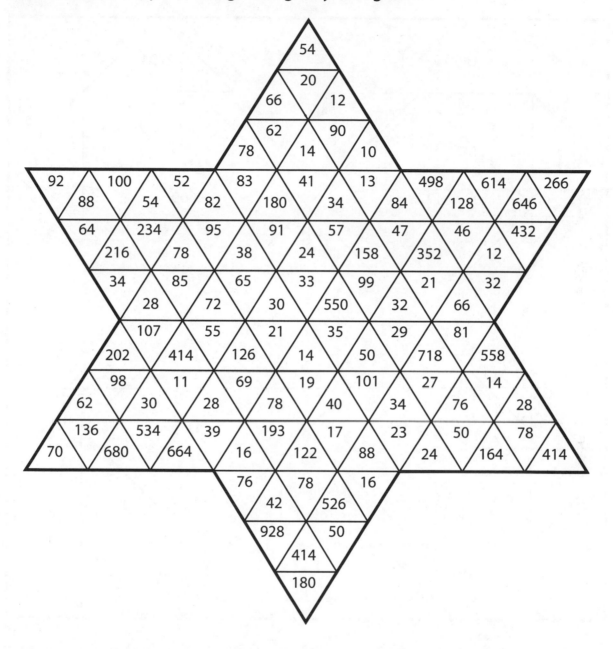

If the number is	Color the shape
even	blue
odd	yellow

Quilt Math   Scholastic Professional Books

 Extra! Guess how many of the smallest triangles there are in the quilt block.
Then count them. Write both numbers on the back of this page.

Name_____

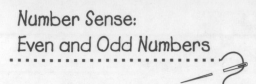

T-Quilt

This quilt block is made from triangles and squares. Can you find these shapes?

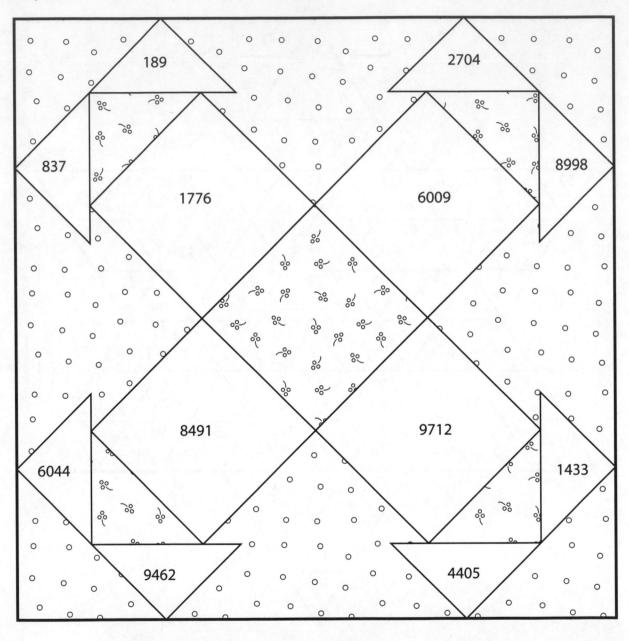

189   2704

837   8998

1776   6009

8491   9712

6044   1433

9462   4405

If the number is	Color the shape
even	blue
odd	yellow

Fill in the other shapes with colors of your choice.

Quilt Math   Scholastic Professional Books

 On the back of this page, write the number of sides a triangle has. Then write the number of sides a square and rectangle have.

Name_____

Checkerboard

Quilt patterns were often named after favorite games or pastimes. This one
was named after the game board pioneers used to play Checkers.

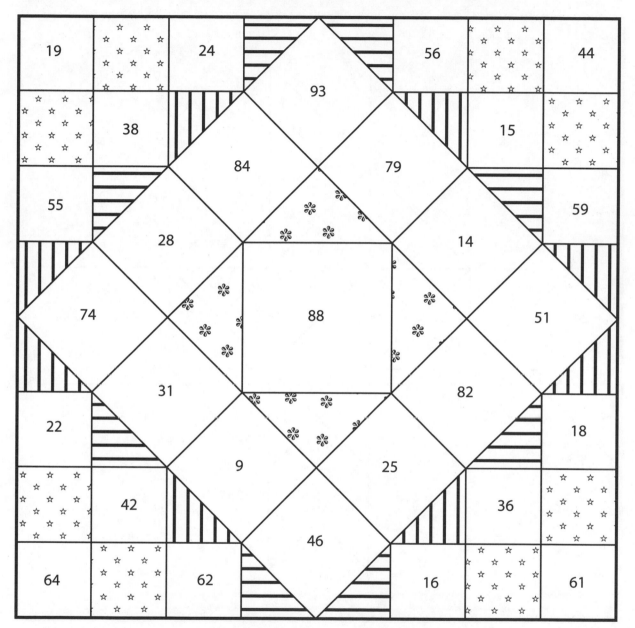

Round each number to the nearest ten.

If the number rounds to	Color the shape
10, 30, or 80	yellow
20, 40, or 60	green
50, 70, or 90	orange

Fill in the other
shapes with
colors of your
choice.

Extra! Circle all of the numbers that round to 20.
11 12 13 14 15 16 17 18 19 20 21 22 23 24 25 26 27 28 29

Quilt Math   Scholastic Professional Books

Name_____

Diamond Cross

In the early 1800s people began to hold county fairs. At the fairs, prizes were given for the best quilts.

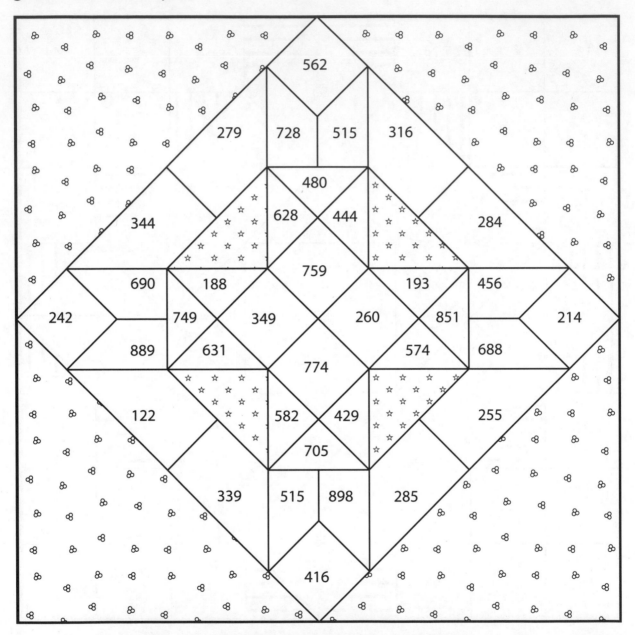

Round each number to the nearest hundred.

If the number rounds to	Color the shape
100, 300, or 800	purple
200, 400, or 600	black
500, 700, or 900	pink

Fill in the other shapes with colors of your choice.

Extra! On the back of this page, write six numbers that round to 800.

Quilt Math   Scholastic Professional Books

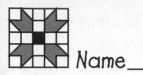

Name_____

Star in a Diamond

There are 20 triangles in this quilt block that are the same size. Can you find them all?

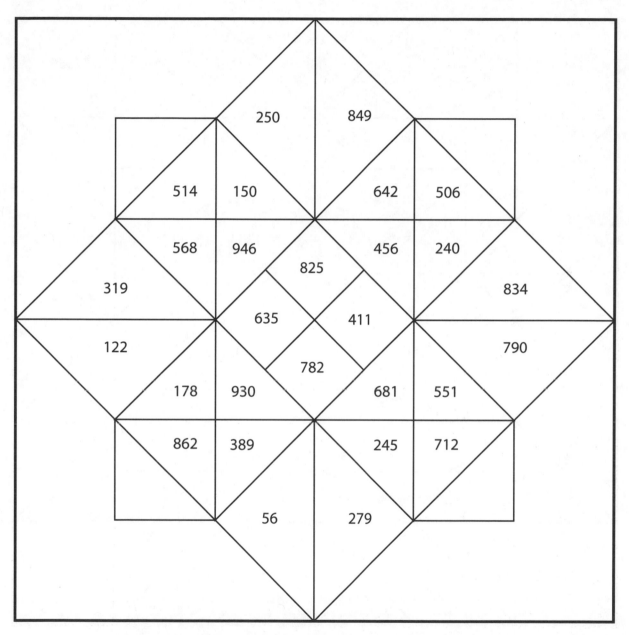

Round each number to the nearest hundred.

If the number rounds to	Color the shape
100, 300, or 800	dark blue
200, 400, or 600	yellow
500, 700, or 900	pink

Fill in the other shapes with colors of your choice.

Quilt Math   Scholastic Professional Books

 Extra! On the back of this page, write four numbers that round to 600. Then write four numbers between 500 and 700 that do not round to 600.

Name_____

Fly Away

In 1854 the sewing machine was first used in the home. Before that time, people sewed all quilts by hand.

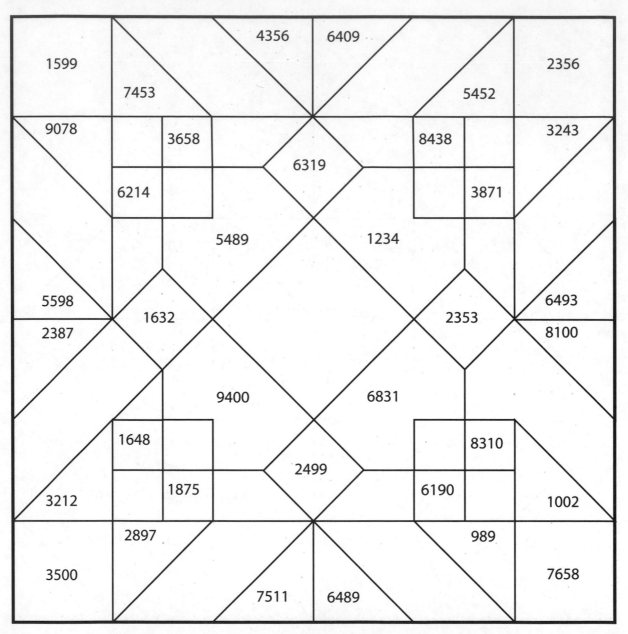

1599   4356   6409   2356
7453   5452
9078   3658   8438   3243
6214   6319   3871
5489   1234
5598   6493
2387   1632   2353   8100
9400   6831
1648   8310
2499
3212   1875   6190   1002
2897   989
3500   7658
7511   6489

Round each number to the nearest thousand.

If the number rounds to	Color the shape
1000, 3000, 5000, 7000, or 9000	red
2000, 4000, 6000, or 8000	green

Fill in the other shapes with colors of your choice.

 Extra! On the back of this page, write four numbers between 7000 and 9000 that do not round to 8000.

Quilt Math   Scholastic Professional Books

Name_____

Busy Sidewalks

During the Civil War, many soldiers did not have blankets. Family members made quilts for the soldiers and sent them to the battlefield.

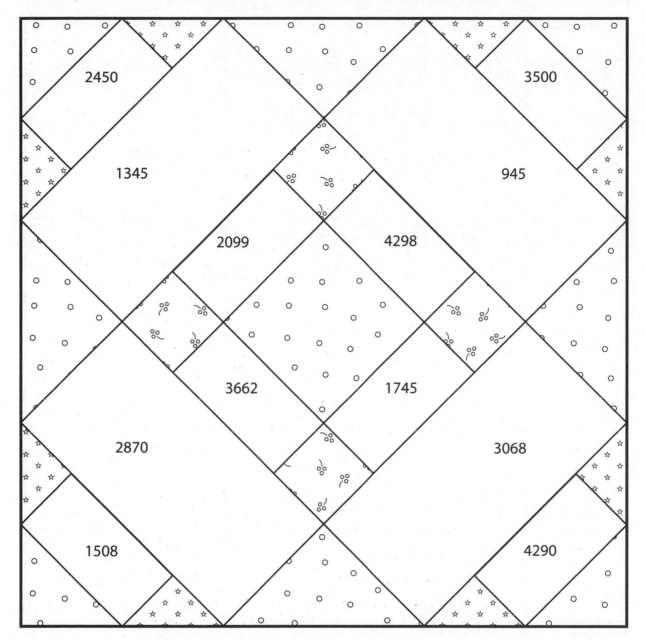

Round each number to the nearest thousand.

If the number rounds to	Color the shape
1000 or 3000	yellow
2000 or 4000	black

Fill in the other shapes with colors of your choice.

Extra! Draw a rectangle. Then draw the same rectangle turned.

Quilt Math Scholastic Professional Books

57

Name_____

Prosperity

In pioneer days, quilting was both fun and work. It was fun to piece the colored shapes together to create a design, and work to hand-sew the pieces.

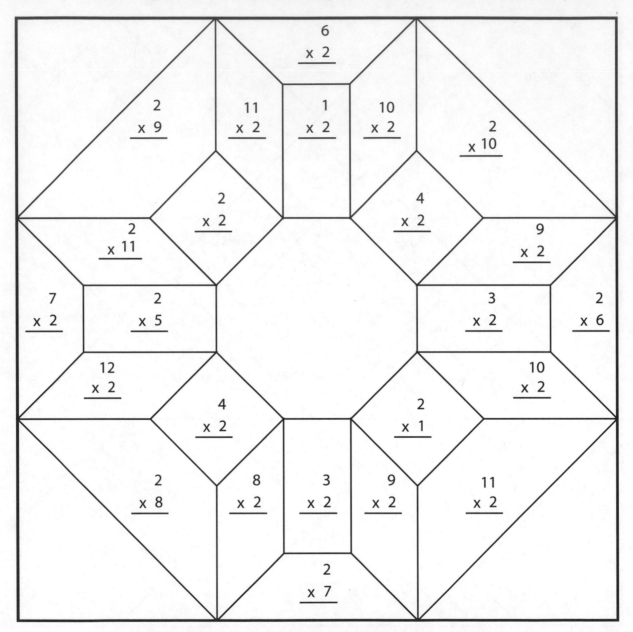

Solve the problems.

If the answer is between	Color the shape
1 and 10	blue
11 and 14	red
15 and 24	yellow

Fill in the other shapes with colors of your choice.

Quilt Math Scholastic Professional Books

Extra! Circle the shapes that are in this quilt block.
square   triangle   rectangle   circle   octagon

58

Name_____

Party Hats

To protect their fingers, quilters place thimbles on their thumbs and use them to push the end of the threaded needle through the fabric.

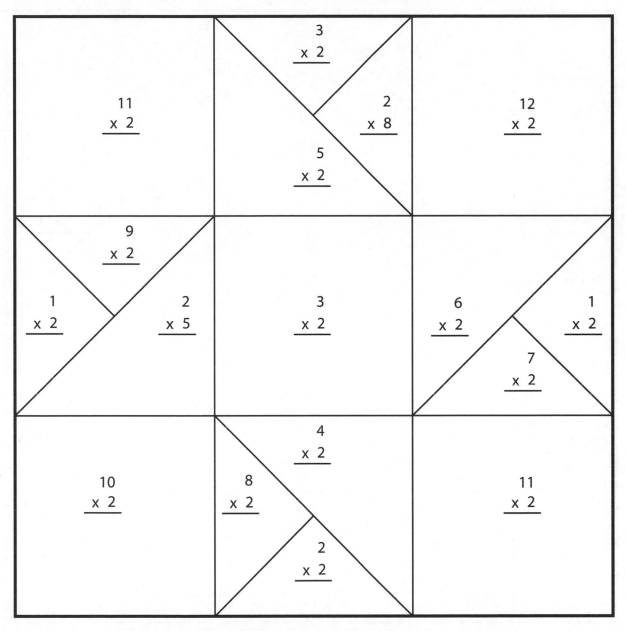

Solve the problems.

If the answer is between	Color the shape
1 and 6	green
7 and 12	black
13 and 18	blue
19 and 24	brown

 Four sets of twins are playing baseball. How many children is that? Write your answer on the back of this page.

Quilt Math Scholastic Professional Books

Name_____

Weathervane

This pattern is named Weathervane. Weathervanes move with the wind and show the direction the wind is coming from.

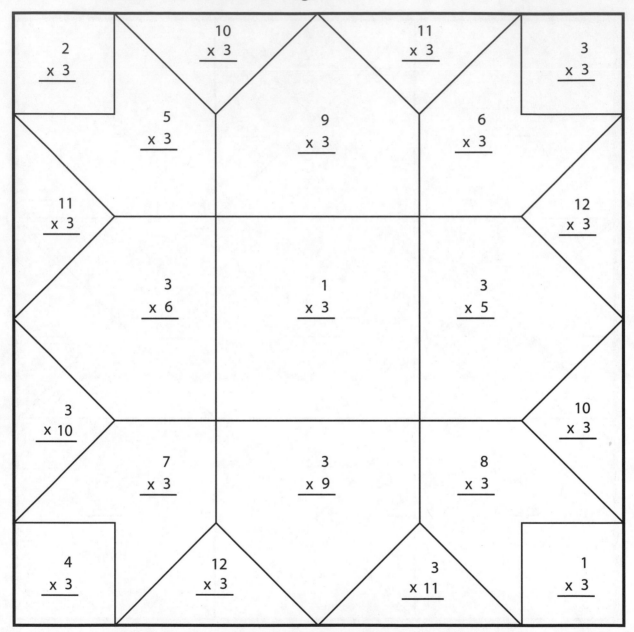

Solve the problems.

If the answer is between	Color the shape
1 and 12	dark pink
13 and 28	yellow
29 and 36	green

 A tricycle has three wheels. On the back of this page, write how many wheels five tricycles have.

Quilt Math · Scholastic Professional Books

 Name_____

 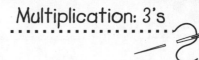

Swing in the Center

This quilt block was named after a square dance of the same name.

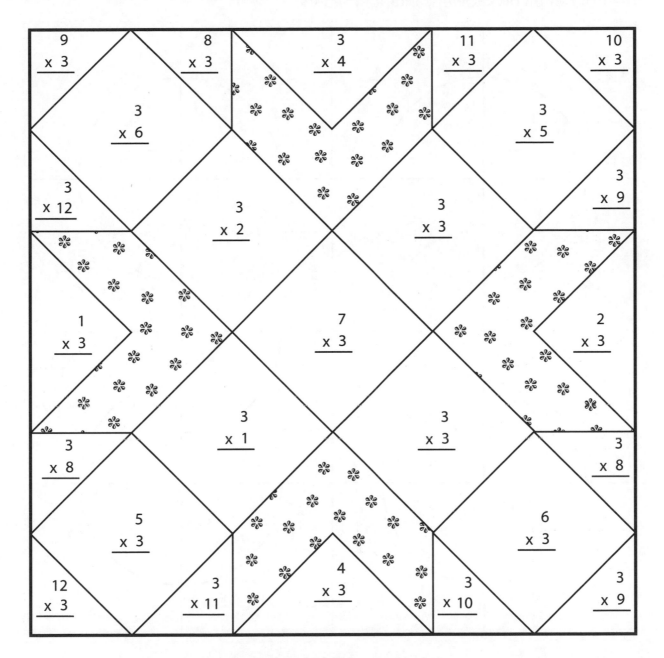

| 9 | 8 | 3 | 11 | 10 |
| x 3 | x 3 | x 4 | x 3 | x 3 |

3
x 6

3
x 5

3
x 12

3
x 2

3
x 3

3
x 9

1
x 3

7
x 3

2
x 3

3
x 8

3
x 1

3
x 3

3
x 8

5
x 3

4
x 3

6
x 3

| 12 | 3 | 4 | 3 | 3 |
| x 3 | x 11 | x 3 | x 10 | x 9 |

Solve the problems.

If the answer is between	Color the shape
1 and 12	green
13 and 22	yellow
23 and 37	blue

Fill in the other shapes with colors of your choice. CRAYON

Quilt Math   Scholastic Professional Books

 Triplets are three children who are born together. On the back of this page, write how many children are in six sets of triplets.

61

Name_____

Wonder of the World

Quilt blocks aren't just sewn together to make quilts. They are often placed on the front of pillows, towels, and pot holders.

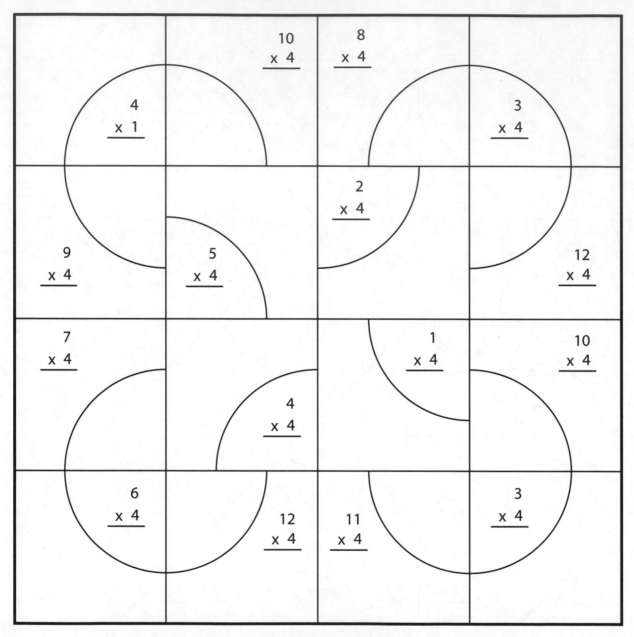

Solve the problems.

If the answer is between	Color the shape
1 and 24	light blue
25 and 48	yellow

Fill in the other shapes with colors of your choice.

 Extra! A car has four tires. On the back of this page, write how many tires eight cars have.

Quilt Math   Scholastic Professional Books

Name_____

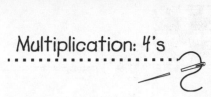

King Tut's Crown

Each of the sixteen squares in this block contain the same curved shape.
The squares have been flipped or turned to create the design.

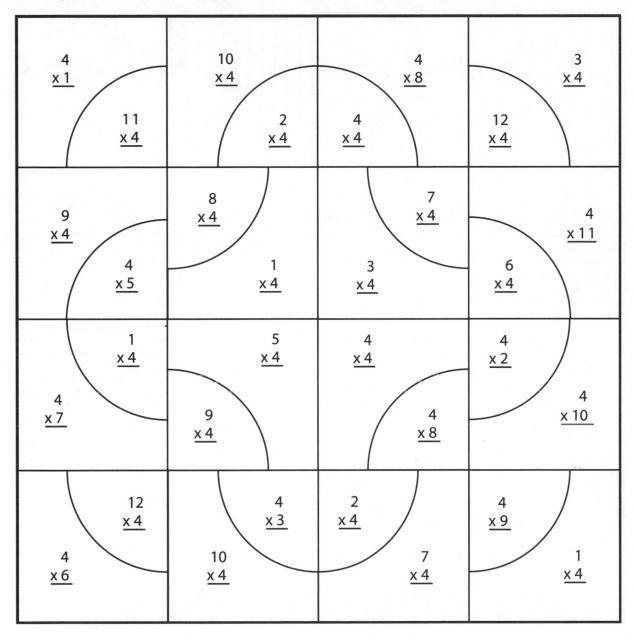

Row 1:
4 x 1   10 x 4   4 x 8   3 x 4
11 x 4   2 x 4   4 x 4   12 x 4

Row 2:
9 x 4   8 x 4   7 x 4   4 x 11
4 x 5   1 x 4   3 x 4   6 x 4

Row 3:
1 x 4   5 x 4   4 x 4   4 x 2
4 x 7   9 x 4   4 x 8   4 x 10

Row 4:
12 x 4   4 x 3   2 x 4   4 x 9
4 x 6   10 x 4   7 x 4   1 x 4

Solve the problems.

If the answer is between	Color the shape
1 and 24	green
25 and 48	yellow

 Extra! Skip count by 4's from 4 to 48. Write the numbers on the back of this page.

Quilt Math   Scholastic Professional Books

Name_____

Around the World

In the 1920s it was popular to create quilts with just two or three colors like this quilt block. One of the colors was often white.

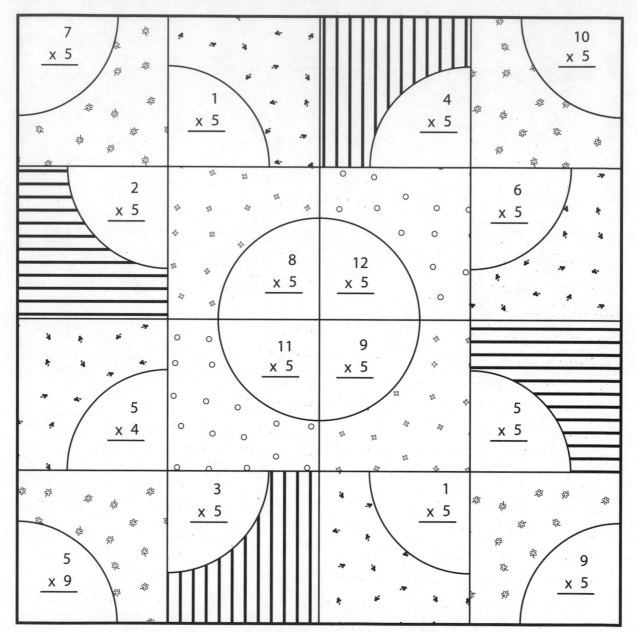

Solve the problems.

If the answer is between	Color the shape
1 and 30	pink
31 and 60	light blue

Fill in the other shapes with colors of your choice.

 Extra! Skip count by 5's from 5 to 60. Write the numbers on the back of this page.

Quilt Math   Scholastic Professional Books

Name_____

Love's Ring Nonesuch

In the early days, quilt patterns were so hard to find that they were traded from person to person.

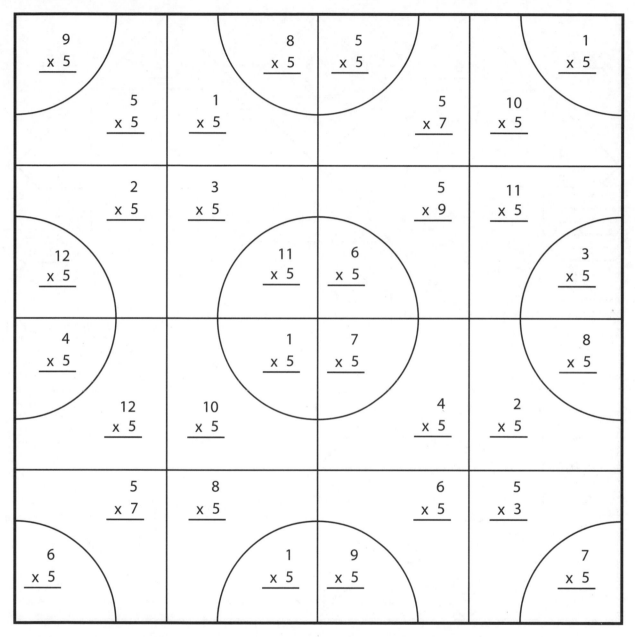

9 x 5		8 x 5	5 x 5		1 x 5
5 x 5	1 x 5		5 x 7	10 x 5	
2 x 5	3 x 5		5 x 9	11 x 5	
12 x 5		11 x 5	6 x 5		3 x 5
4 x 5		1 x 5	7 x 5		8 x 5
12 x 5	10 x 5			4 x 5	2 x 5
5 x 7	8 x 5		6 x 5	5 x 3	
6 x 5		1 x 5	9 x 5		7 x 5

Solve the problems.

If the answer is between	Color the shape
1 and 30	green
31 and 60	red

 Extra! Fill in the missing numbers.

5, ____, 15, ____, 25, 30, ____, 40, 45, 50, ____

Quilt Math   Scholastic Professional Books

Name_____

 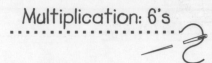
Farmer's Field

Three triangles of different sizes are used in this quilt pattern. Can you find them all?

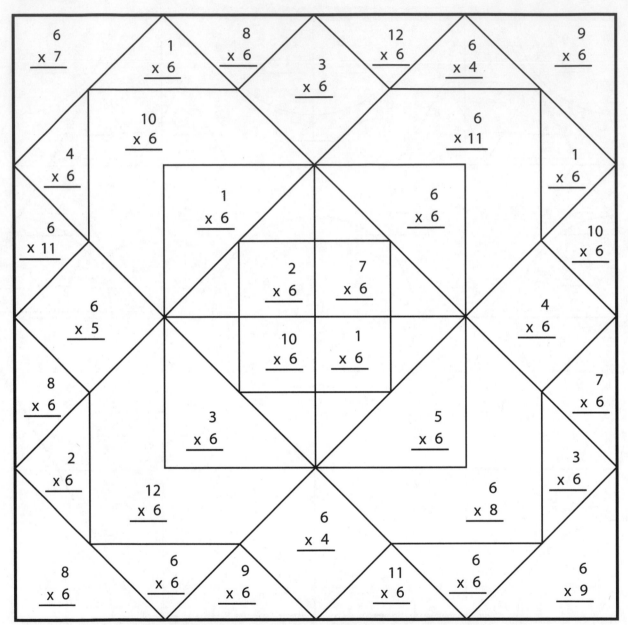

Solve the problems.

If the answer is between	Color the shape
1 and 41	brown
42 and 72	green

Fill in the other shapes with colors of your choice.

Extra! Adam has six paper bags. He wants to put eight pretzels in each bag. How many pretzels will he need in all? Write the answer on the back of this page.

Quilt Math   Scholastic Professional Books

Name_____

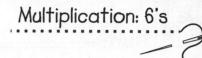

Flat Iron Patchwork

This quilt block has 54 triangles. Can you find them all?

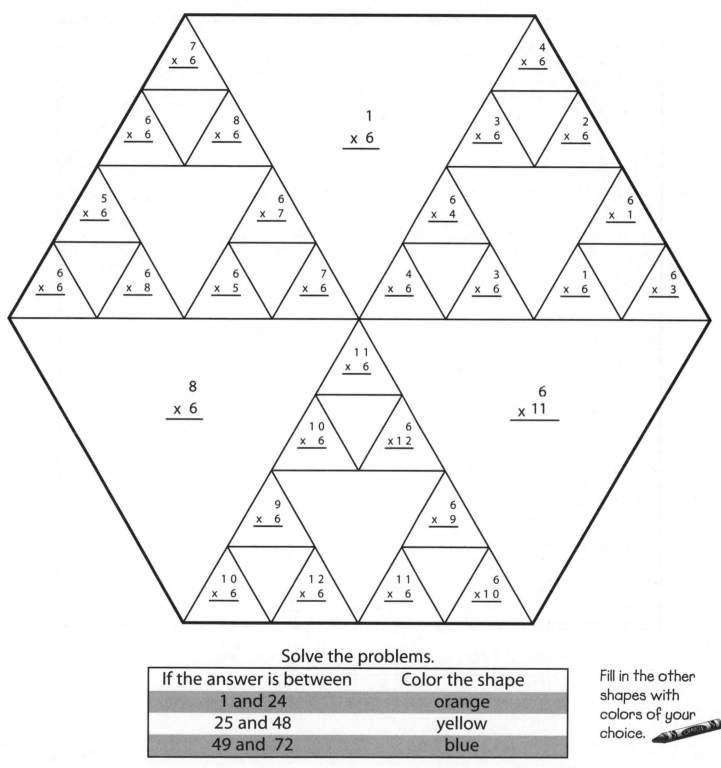

Quilt Math   Scholastic Professional Books

Solve the problems.

If the answer is between	Color the shape
1 and 24	orange
25 and 48	yellow
49 and 72	blue

Fill in the other shapes with colors of your choice.

 On the back of this page, write how many different sizes of triangles there are in this quilt block.

67

Name_____

Illusion

In the 1920s, signature quilt blocks were popular. Women sewed their names and birth dates on the quilt blocks they made.

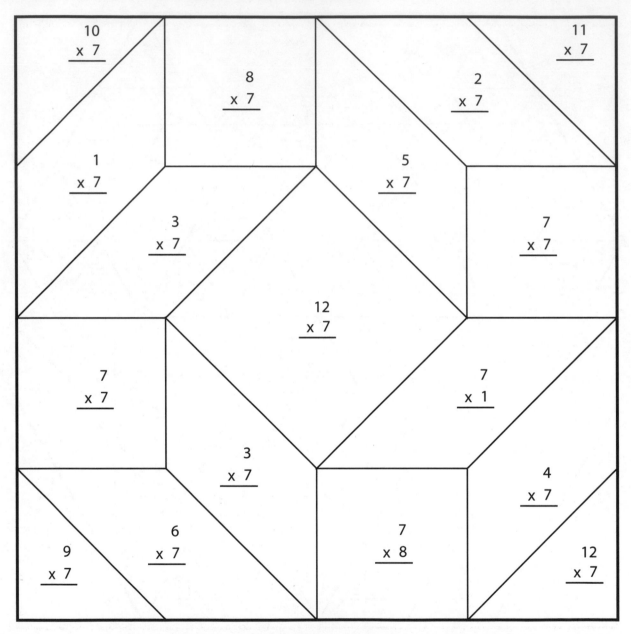

Solve the problems.

If the answer is between	Color the shape
1 and 42	pink
43 and 56	dark pink
57 and 84	blue

 On the back of this page, write a multiplication fact with one factor that is 7.

Quilt Math Scholastic Professional Books

68

Name_____

Spiral Cross

During the Civil War, women made quilts in memory of lost sons, brothers, and husbands. Sometimes, they included scraps of their loved ones' clothes.

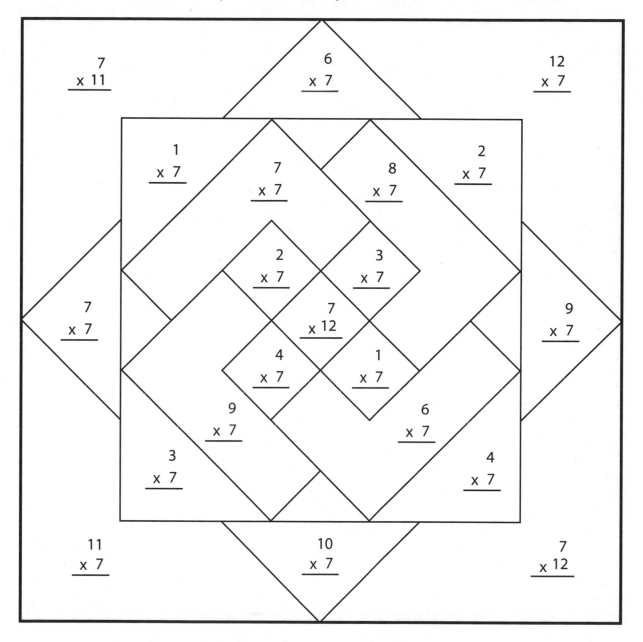

7
x 11

6
x 7

12
x 7

1
x 7

7
x 7

8
x 7

2
x 7

2
x 7

3
x 7

7
x 7

7
x 12

9
x 7

4
x 7

1
x 7

9
x 7

6
x 7

3
x 7

4
x 7

11
x 7

10
x 7

7
x 12

Solve the problems.

If the answer is between	Color the shape
1 and 28	black
29 and 76	orange
77 and 84	green

Fill in the other shapes with colors of your choice.

Quilt Math   Scholastic Professional Books

Extra! Skip count by 7's from 7 to 84. Write the numbers on the back of this page.

Name_____

Windmills and Stars

This quilt block has a windmill and a star in it. Can you find them both?

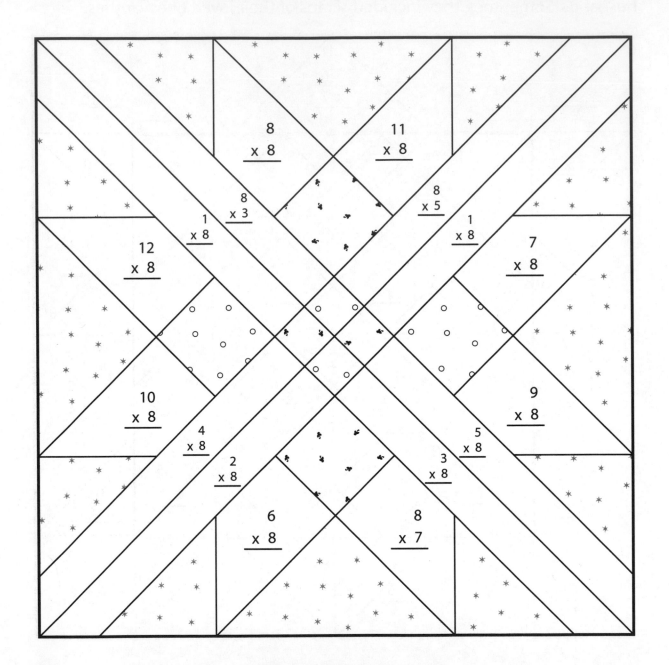

Quilt Math Scholastic Professional Books

Solve the problems.

If the answer is between	Color the shape
1 and 40	green
41 and 96	yellow

Fill in the other shapes with colors of your choice.

 Extra! Skip count by 8's from 8 to 96. Write the numbers on the back of this page.

Name_____

Beams of Light

Some quilts are made to show things from nature like trees, flowers, apples, or beams of light.

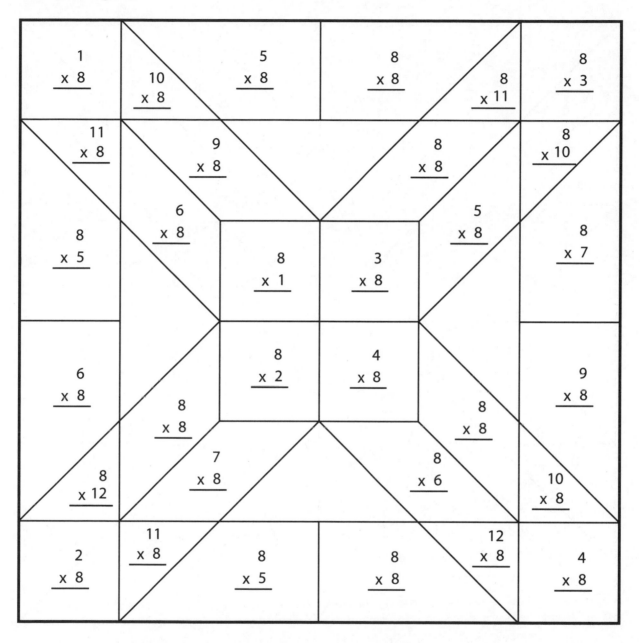

1 x 8	10 x 8	5 x 8	8 x 8	8 x 11	8 x 3
11 x 8	9 x 8		8 x 8		8 x 10
8 x 5	6 x 8	8 x 1	3 x 8	5 x 8	8 x 7
6 x 8	8 x 8	8 x 2	4 x 8	8 x 8	9 x 8
8 x 12	7 x 8		8 x 6		10 x 8
2 x 8	11 x 8	8 x 5	8 x 8	12 x 8	4 x 8

Solve the problems.

If the answer is between	Color the shape
1 and 32	yellow
33 and 79	light blue
80 and 96	green

Fill in the other shapes with colors of your choice.

Extra! On the back of this page, write the names of three shapes that you see in this quilt.

Quilt Math Scholastic Professional Books

Name_____

Night and Day

During the Great Depression, quilts were raffled to raise money for people who were poor or sick.

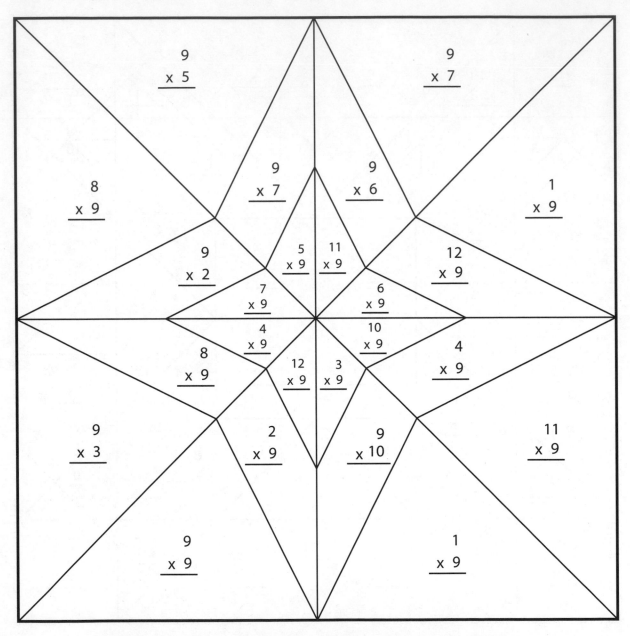

Solve the problems.

If the answer is between	Color the shape
1 and 54	blue
55 and 108	yellow

 Skip count by 9's from 9 to 108. Write the numbers on the back of this page.

Quilt Math   Scholastic Professional Books

Name_____

Dakota Sun

This design was made in the American Southwest in 1826.

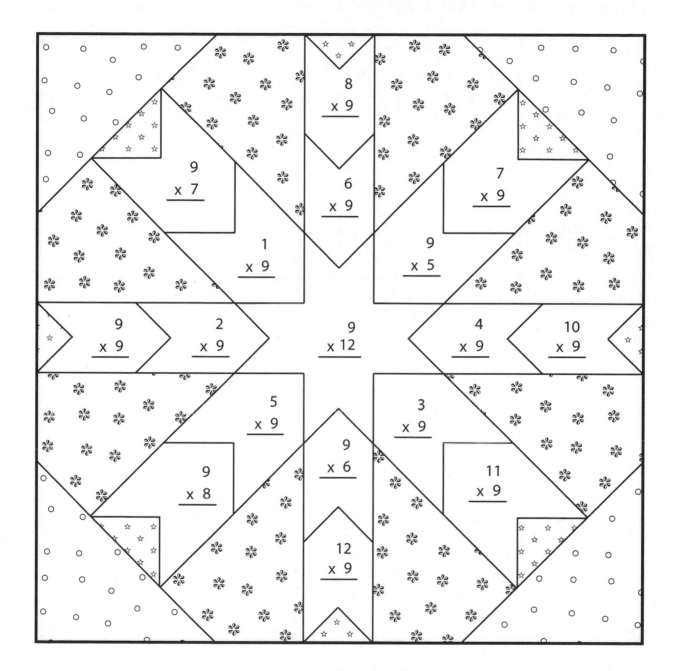

Problems shown in the quilt design:

8 × 9

9 × 7

6 × 9

7 × 9

1 × 9

9 × 5

9 × 9   2 × 9   9 × 12   4 × 9   10 × 9

5 × 9   3 × 9

9 × 8   9 × 6   11 × 9

12 × 9

Solve the problems.

If the answer is between	Color the shape
1 and 54	orange
55 and 108	brown

Fill in the other shapes with colors of your choice.

 Adam is thinking of an even number less than 36 that is a multiple of 9. Write the number on the back of this page.

Quilt Math   Scholastic Professional Books

73

Name_____

Rows of Bows

In this quilt block, two triangles have been placed together to make a bow shape. Can you find all four bows?

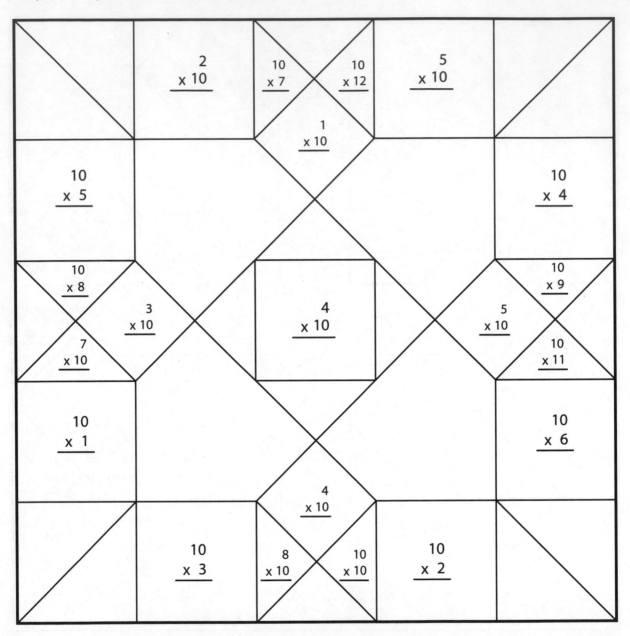

Solve the problems.

If the answer is between	Color the shape
0 and 60	purple
61 and 120	yellow

Fill in the other shapes with colors of your choice.

 Extra! On the back of this page, draw a picture of two triangles placed together to make a bow shape.

Quilt Math Scholastic Professional Books

Name_____

Twirling Triangles

Why do you think this quilt block is called Twirling Triangles?

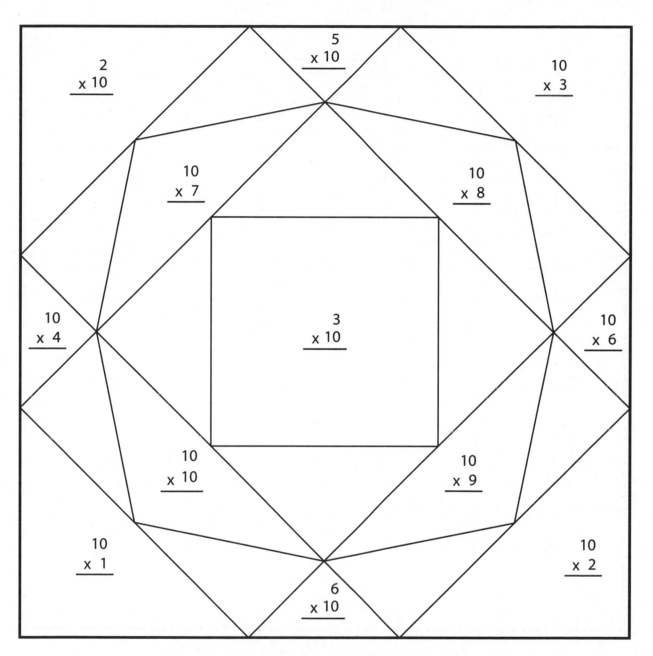

Solve the problems.

If the answer is between	Color the shape
1 and 30	yellow
31 and 70	orange
71 and 100	dark blue

Fill in the other shapes with colors of your choice.

Extra On the back of this page, write your age. Multiply it by 10.

Name_____

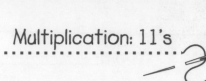

Sparkling Diamond

In colonial times, New England women made quilted petticoats.

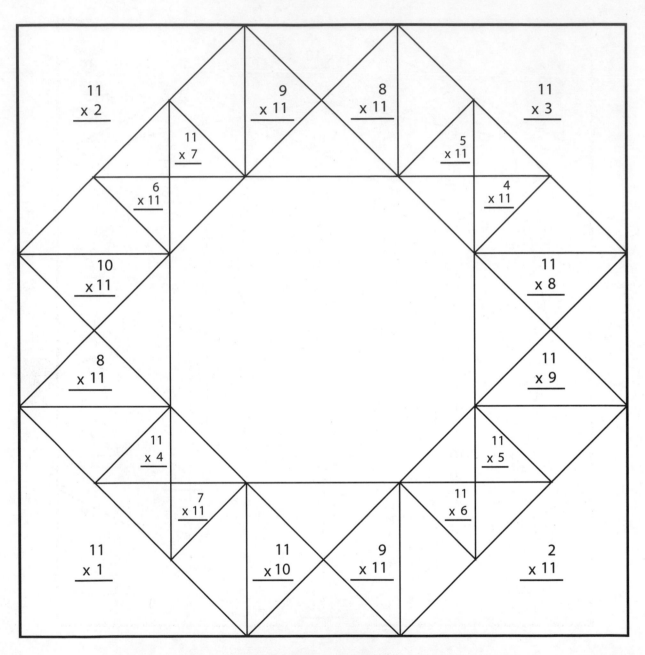

Solve the problems.

If the answer is between	Color the shape
1 and 40	dark red
41 and 80	blue
81 and 120	gray

Fill in the other shapes with colors of your choice.

Quilt Math   Scholastic Professional Books

 Extra! On the back of this page, write three multiplication facts that each have one factor of 11 and an even product.

Name_____

Patchwork Cube

In the 1930s, flour, sugar, fertilizer, animal feed, and seeds were sold in colorful cloth sacks. The sacks were then cut into shapes and used to make quilts.

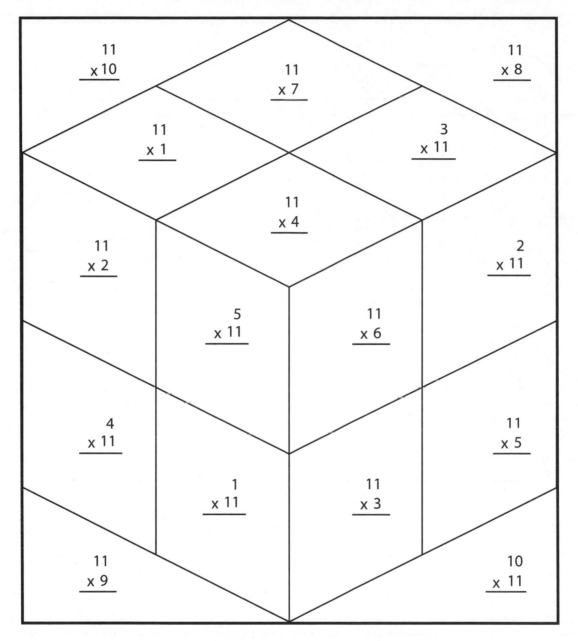

Solve the problems.

If the answer is between	Color the shape
1 and 40	yellow
41 and 80	dark green
81 and 120	dark red

 On the back of this page, write three multiplication facts that each have one factor of 11 and an odd product.

Quilt Math   Scholastic Professional Books

Name_____

Double X

Some quilters sew fabric labels on the backs of their quilts. They write the name of the person who made it, who it was made for, and the date.

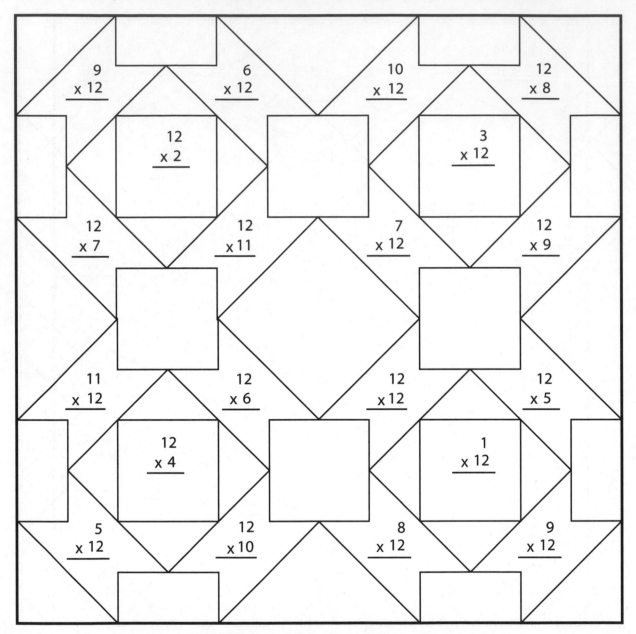

Solve the problems.

If the answer is between	Color the shape
1 and 48	black
49 and 96	dark blue
97 and 144	dark purple

Fill in the other shapes with colors of your choice.

Extra! On the back of this page, multiply your age by 12.

Quilt Math   Scholastic Professional Books

Name_____

Diamond Checkerboard

Guess how many diamonds are in this quilt pattern. Then count them to find the exact number.

Multiply each number by 12.

If the answer is between	Color the shape
12 and 60	red
61 and 144	black

Fill in the other shapes with colors of your choice.

 Circle all of the numbers that are multiples of 12.

11 12 24 36 48 49 60 72 84 90 96 108 120 132 144 148

Quilt Math   Scholastic Professional Books

79

Name_____

Wagon Wheel

In pioneer days, some families had one fancy quilt that was used only on special days, such as holidays or birthdays.

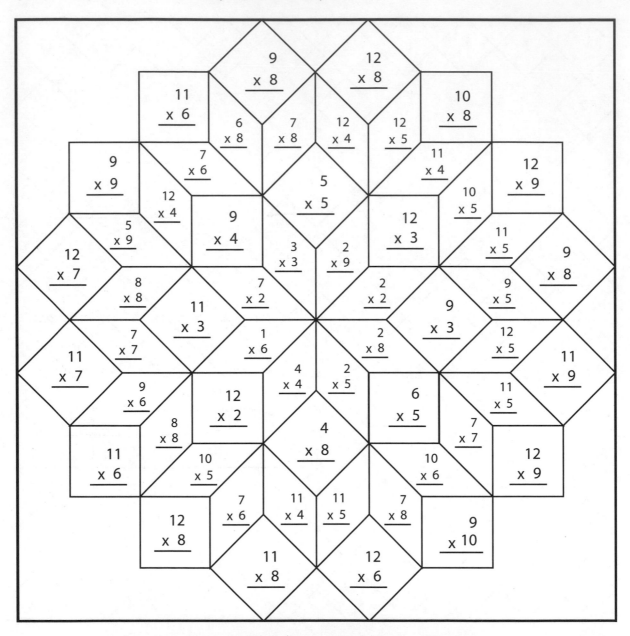

Solve the problems.

If the answer is between	Color the shape
0 and 20	light pink
21 and 40	dark pink
41 and 65	light blue
66 and 108	dark blue

Fill in the other shapes with colors of your choice.

Quilt Math   Scholastic Professional Books

 Extra! If someone were twice as old as you are, how old would that person be? Write your answer on the back of this page.

Name_____

Chinese Lantern

Many different kinds of quilt patterns are made to look like Chinese lanterns.

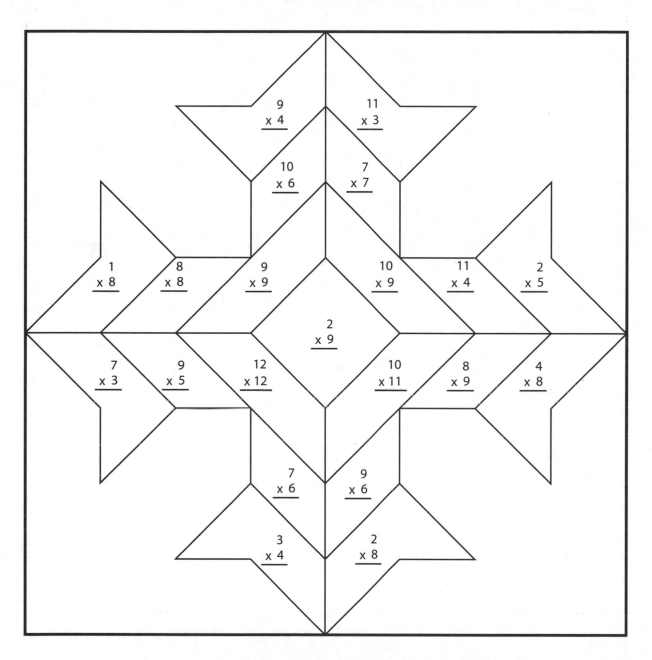

Solve the problems.

If the answer is between	Color the shape
0 and 40	black
41 and 80	pink
81 and 144	purple

Fill in the other shapes with colors of your choice.

 On the back of this page, write three multiplication problems that each have a product of 12.

Quilt Math   Scholastic Professional Books

81

Name_____

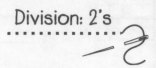

Sailboat

Do you see the sailboat in this quilt block? The sails are made from triangles.
The boat is made from squares and triangles.

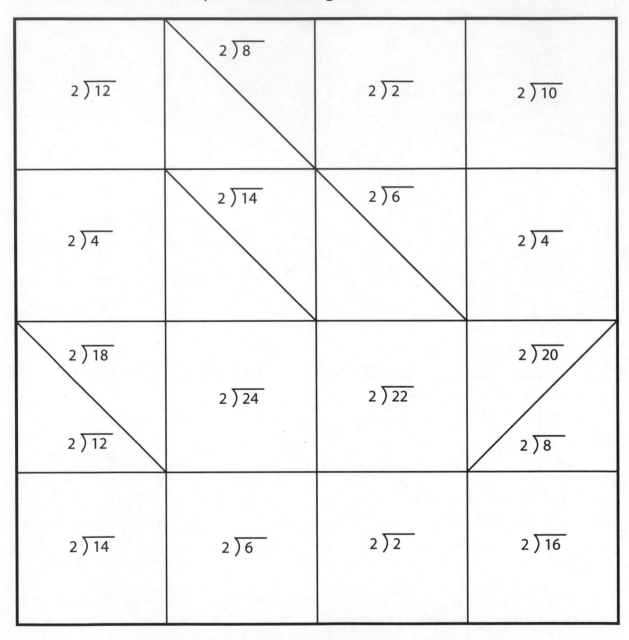

Solve the problems.

If the answer is between	Color the shape
1 and 8	blue
9 and 12	orange

 Extra! On the back of this page, draw an object such as a kite or book using both squares and triangles.

Quilt Math   Scholastic Professional Books

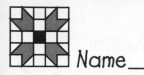
Name_____

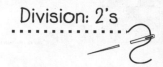

Cactus Basket

In colonial days, families needed lots of quilts in the winter. Family members each used three or four quilts on their beds to keep warm.

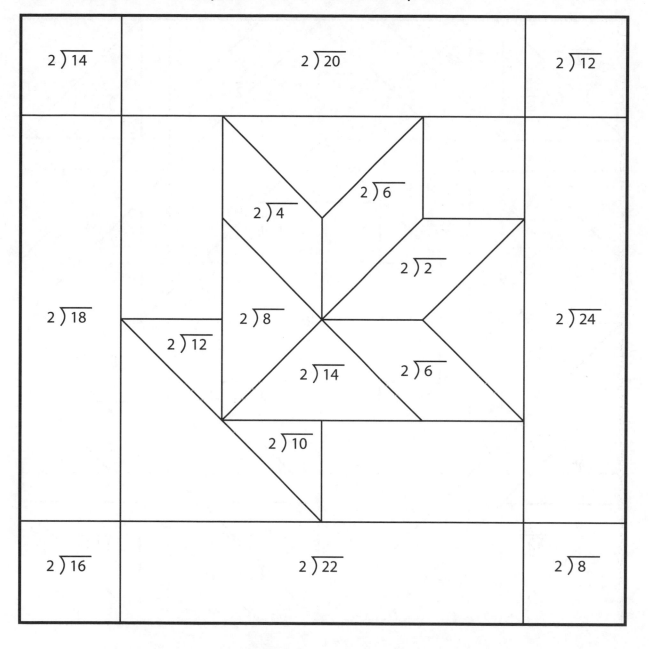

$2\overline{)14}$ $2\overline{)20}$ $2\overline{)12}$

$2\overline{)6}$ $2\overline{)4}$ $2\overline{)2}$

$2\overline{)18}$ $2\overline{)8}$ $2\overline{)24}$

$2\overline{)12}$ $2\overline{)14}$ $2\overline{)6}$

$2\overline{)10}$

$2\overline{)16}$ $2\overline{)22}$ $2\overline{)8}$

Solve the problems.

If the answer is between	Color the shape
1 and 3	yellow
4 and 8	green
9 and 12	orange

Fill in the other shapes with colors of your choice.

Extra! On the back of this page, write a division problem that has a divisor of 2.

Quilt Math   Scholastic Professional Books

Name_____

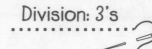

Navajo Rug

In the 1800s, Navajo women made quilt blocks similar to this one. The colors red, black, and gray were commonly used in quilts and rugs during that time.

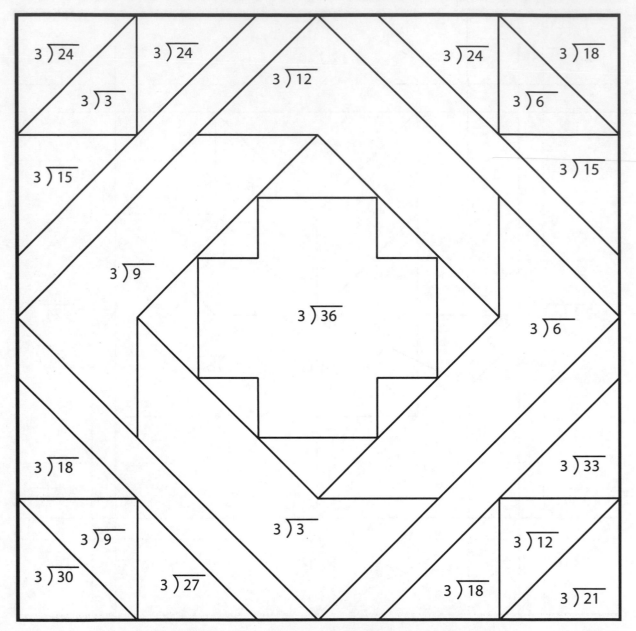

Solve the problems.

If the answer is	Color the shape
between 1 and 4	red
between 5 and 11	gray
12	black

Fill in the other shapes with colors of your choice.

Quilt Math   Scholastic Professional Books

 Three sisters are coloring 12 eggs. If they each color the same number of eggs, how many will each girl color? Write your answer on the back of this page.

Name_____

Sunbeam

Thousands of stitches go into making a quilt. After a quilt top is made, it can take one person many months to quilt all three layers together.

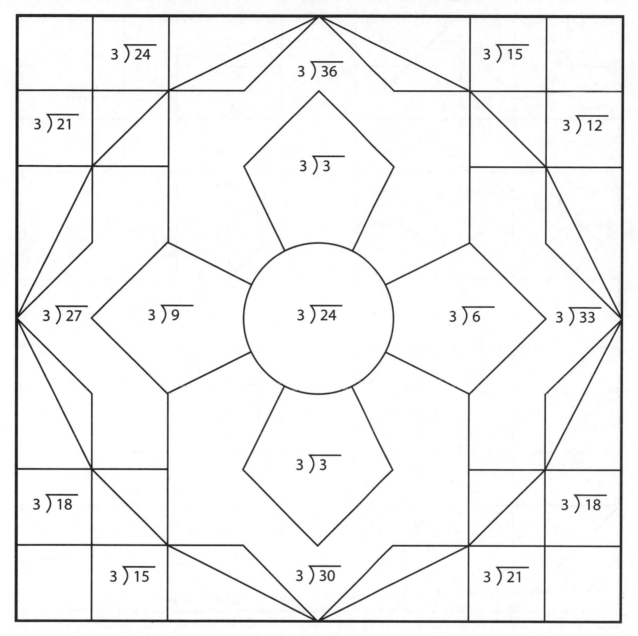

Solve the problems.

If the answer is between	Color the shape
1 and 3	purple
4 and 8	green
9 and 12	pink

Fill in the other shapes with colors of your choice.

 Extra! On the back of this page, write a division word problem and have a friend solve it. Include a picture.

Quilt Math Scholastic Professional Books

85

Name_____

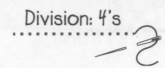

Duck and Duckling

This quilt block is made of three basic shapes. Can you name them?

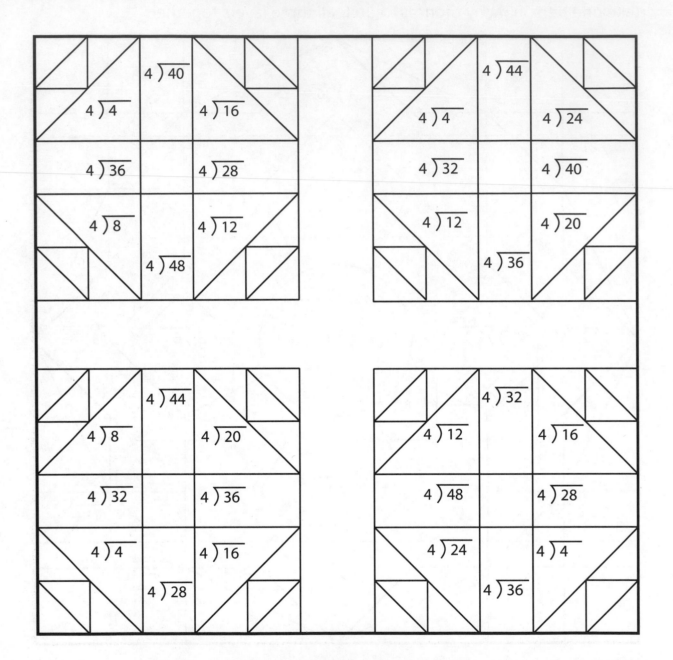

$4\overline{)40}$

$4\overline{)4}$ $4\overline{)16}$

$4\overline{)36}$ $4\overline{)28}$

$4\overline{)8}$ $4\overline{)12}$

$4\overline{)48}$

$4\overline{)44}$

$4\overline{)4}$ $4\overline{)24}$

$4\overline{)32}$ $4\overline{)40}$

$4\overline{)12}$ $4\overline{)20}$

$4\overline{)36}$

$4\overline{)44}$

$4\overline{)8}$ $4\overline{)20}$

$4\overline{)32}$ $4\overline{)36}$

$4\overline{)4}$ $4\overline{)16}$

$4\overline{)28}$

$4\overline{)32}$

$4\overline{)12}$ $4\overline{)16}$

$4\overline{)48}$ $4\overline{)28}$

$4\overline{)24}$ $4\overline{)4}$

$4\overline{)36}$

Solve the problems.

If the answer is between	Color the shape
1 and 6	yellow
7 and 12	orange

Fill in the other shapes with colors of your choice.

Quilt Math Scholastic Professional Books

 Extra! On the back of this page, write the numbers between 1 and 40 that can be evenly divided by 4.

Name_____

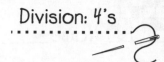

Christmas Star

Some quilts are made to use only on special holidays. This pattern might be used to make a quilt for the Christmas season.

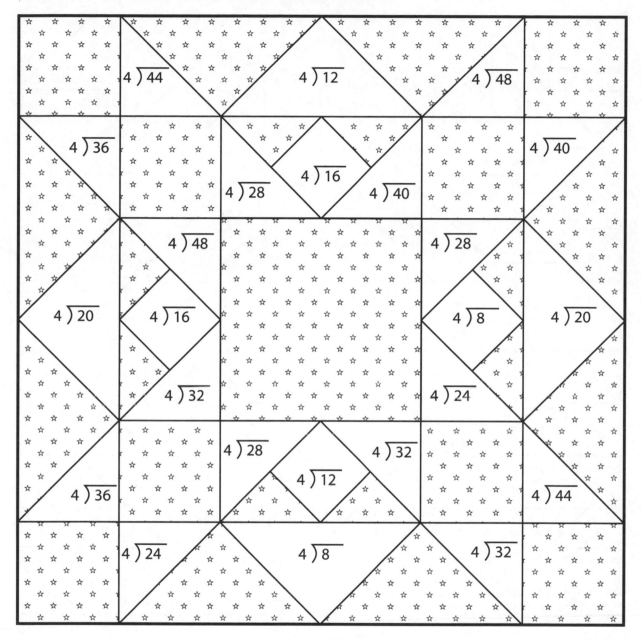

Solve the problems.

If the answer is between	Color the shape
1 and 5	red
6 and 12	green

Fill in the other shapes with colors of your choice.

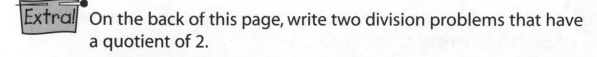

Extra! On the back of this page, write two division problems that have a quotient of 2.

Quilt Math   Scholastic Professional Books

87

Name_____

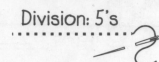

Log Cabin Pineapple

In the 1920s, fabric was bright and colorful. Bubble-gum pink, bright yellow, and mint green were popular colors.

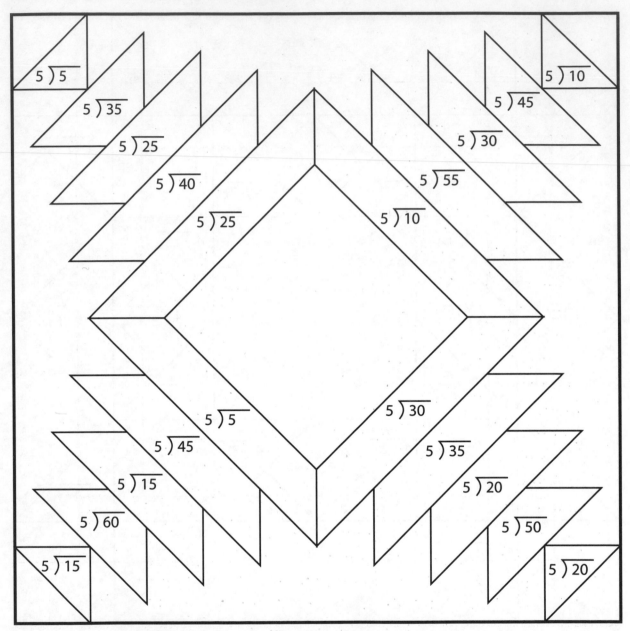

Solve the problems.

If the answer is between	Color the shape
1 and 6	yellow
7 and 12	pink

Fill in the other shapes with colors of your choice.

Extra! On the back of this page, write two division problems that each have a quotient of 5.

Quilt Math   Scholastic Professional Books

Name_____

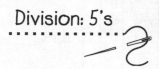

Log Cabin

In pioneer days, the center square in a Log Cabin quilt block was usually red. This showed that the center of the log cabin home was the fireplace.

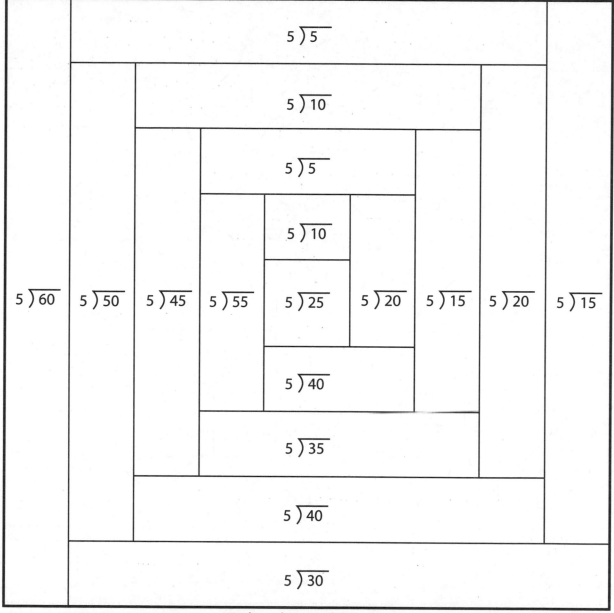

Solve the problems.

If the number is	Color the shape
1 or 2	yellow
3 or 4	green
5	red
between 6 and 8	blue
between 9 and 12	brown

Extra! Twenty children are to be placed in groups of 5 to play a game. On the back of this page, write how many groups there will be in all.

Name_____

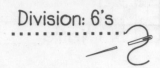

Daisy Days

This quilt pattern is appliqué. The quilter places the fabric daisy on the background, carefully turns under the edges, and sews it in place.

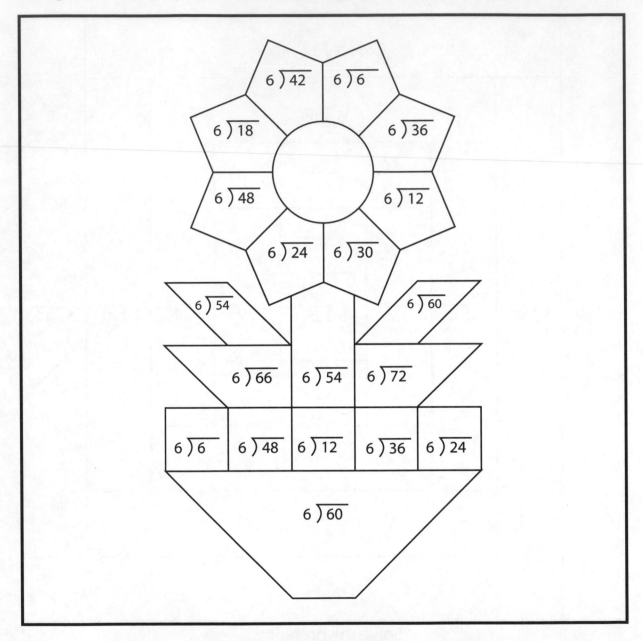

Solve the problems.

If the answer is between	Color the shape
1 and 4	light orange
5 and 8	dark orange
9 and 12	green

Fill in the other shapes with colors of your choice.

 Extra! On the back of this page, write two division problems that have divisors of 6.

Quilt Math Scholastic Professional Books

 Name_____

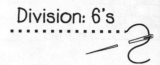

Windstorm

Amish quilt patterns, like this one, are made of simple, solid-colored fabrics and often include the color black.

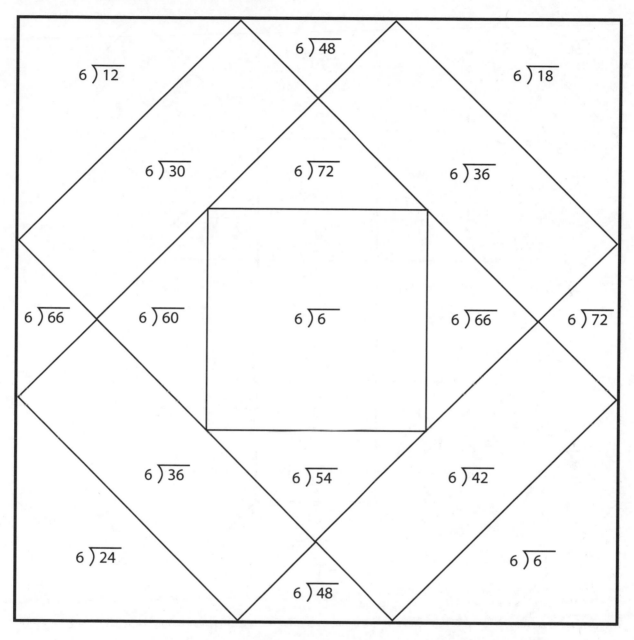

Solve the problems.

If the answer is between	Color the shape
1 and 4	green
5 and 7	black
8 and 12	purple

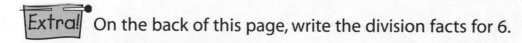 On the back of this page, write the division facts for 6.

Quilt Math Scholastic Professional Books

Name_____

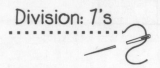

Tiptoes

This square-shaped quilt block is made of nine squares and eight triangles. Can you find them all?

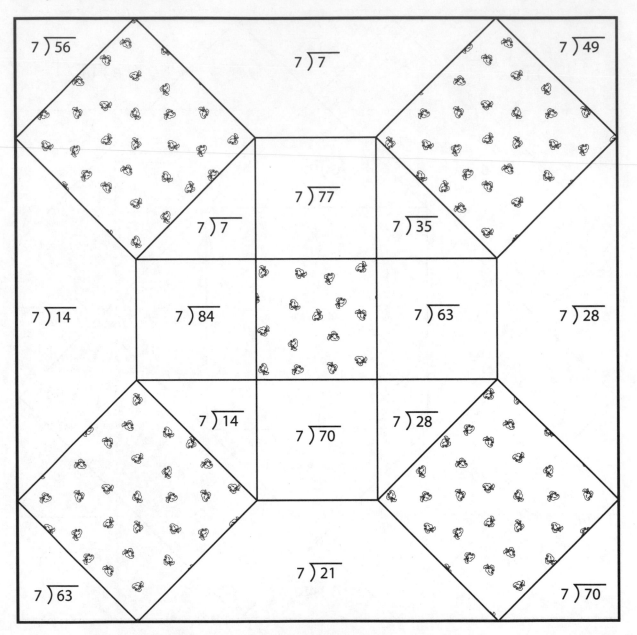

Solve the problems.

If the answer is between	Color the shape
1 and 5	dark pink
6 and 12	yellow

Fill in the other shapes with colors of your choice.

 Extra! On the back of this page, write a division word problem. Have a friend solve it.

92

Quilt Math   Scholastic Professional Books

Name_____

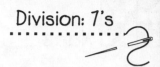

Gold Rush

This quilt block may have gotten its name from the California Gold Rush in 1848.

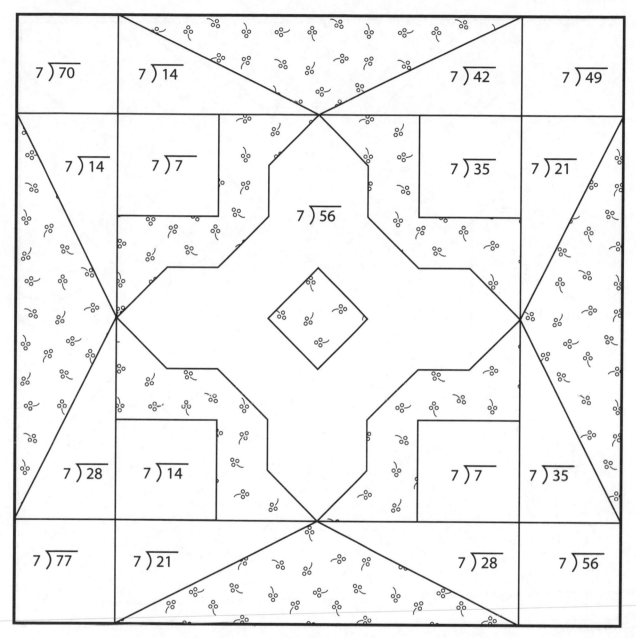

7)70   7)14   7)42   7)49

7)14   7)7   7)35   7)21

7)56

7)28   7)14   7)7   7)35

7)77   7)21   7)28   7)56

Solve the problems.

If the answer is between	Color the shape
1 and 6	purple
7 and 11	yellow

Fill in the other shapes with colors of your choice.

Quilt Math   Scholastic Professional Books

 Extra! On the back of this page, write a division problem that has a divisor of 7 and a quotient of 6.

93

Name_____

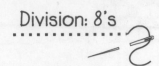

Primrose Path

In pioneer days, there was no electricity, so quilters had to stitch their quilts by candlelight.

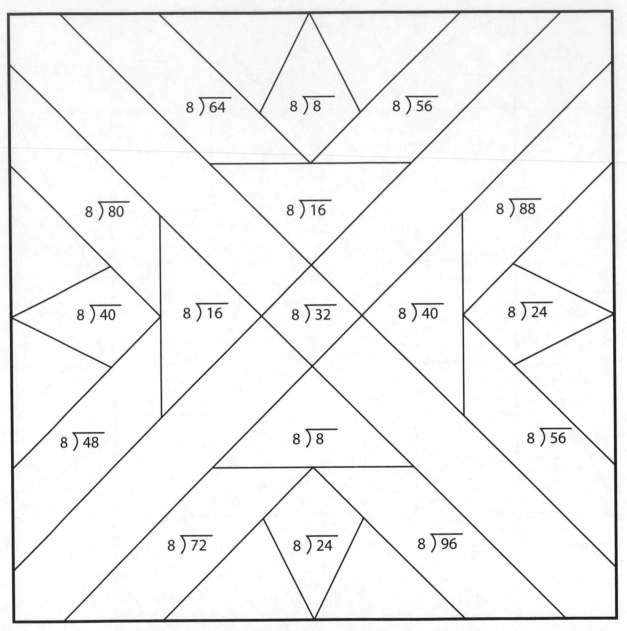

$8\overline{)64}$ $8\overline{)8}$ $8\overline{)56}$

$8\overline{)80}$ $8\overline{)16}$ $8\overline{)88}$

$8\overline{)40}$ $8\overline{)16}$ $8\overline{)32}$ $8\overline{)40}$ $8\overline{)24}$

$8\overline{)48}$ $8\overline{)8}$ $8\overline{)56}$

$8\overline{)72}$ $8\overline{)24}$ $8\overline{)96}$

Quilt Math   Scholastic Professional Books

Solve the problems.

If the answer is between	Color the shape
1 and 5	yellow
6 and 12	green

Fill in the other shapes with colors of your choice.

 Extra! Forty pieces of candy are to be divided evenly among eight bags. On the back of this page, write how many pieces should go in each bag.

Name_____

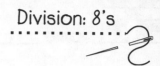

Headdress

Memory quilts are made by taking pieces of fabric from clothes that are special to a person and placing them in a quilt.

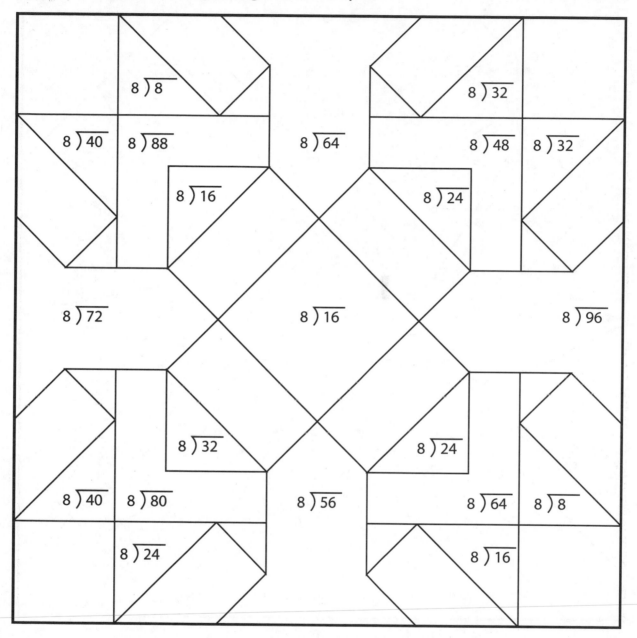

$8\overline{)8}$ $8\overline{)32}$ $8\overline{)40}$ $8\overline{)88}$ $8\overline{)64}$ $8\overline{)48}$ $8\overline{)32}$ $8\overline{)16}$ $8\overline{)24}$ $8\overline{)72}$ $8\overline{)16}$ $8\overline{)96}$ $8\overline{)32}$ $8\overline{)24}$ $8\overline{)40}$ $8\overline{)80}$ $8\overline{)56}$ $8\overline{)64}$ $8\overline{)8}$ $8\overline{)24}$ $8\overline{)16}$

Solve the problems.

If the answer is between	Color the shape
1 and 5	yellow
6 and 12	light green

Fill in the other shapes with colors of your choice.

Quilt Math   Scholastic Professional Books

 Extra! On the back of this page, write two division problems that each have a quotient of 1.

95

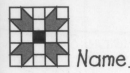

Name_____

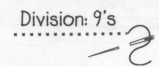

North Carolina Star

There are thousands and thousands of stitches in a handmade quilt. Most people quilt about eight stitches an inch!

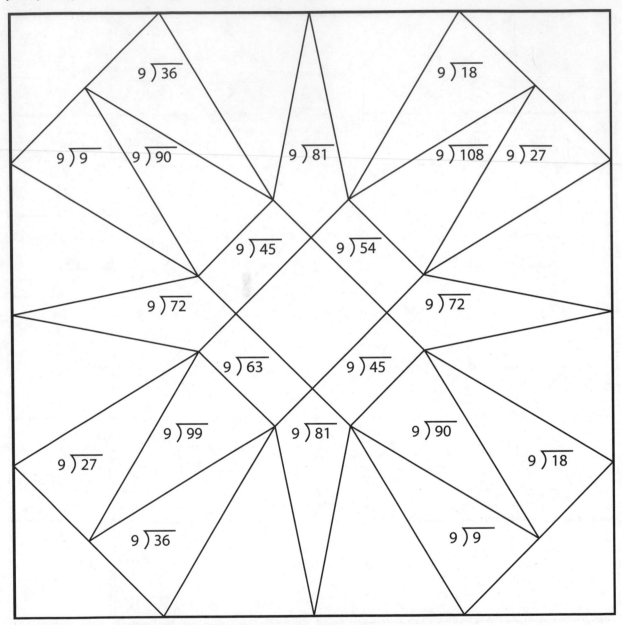

Solve the problems.

If the answer is	Color the shape
between 1 and 4	yellow
between 5 and 7	brown
8 or 9	orange
between 10 and 12	red

Fill in the other shapes with colors of your choice.

Quilt Math   Scholastic Professional Books

Extra! On the back of this page, write two division problems that each have a quotient of 4.

Name_____

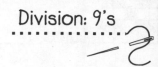

Lace Cloth

In the 1920s and 1930s blue and yellow quilts like this one were very popular.

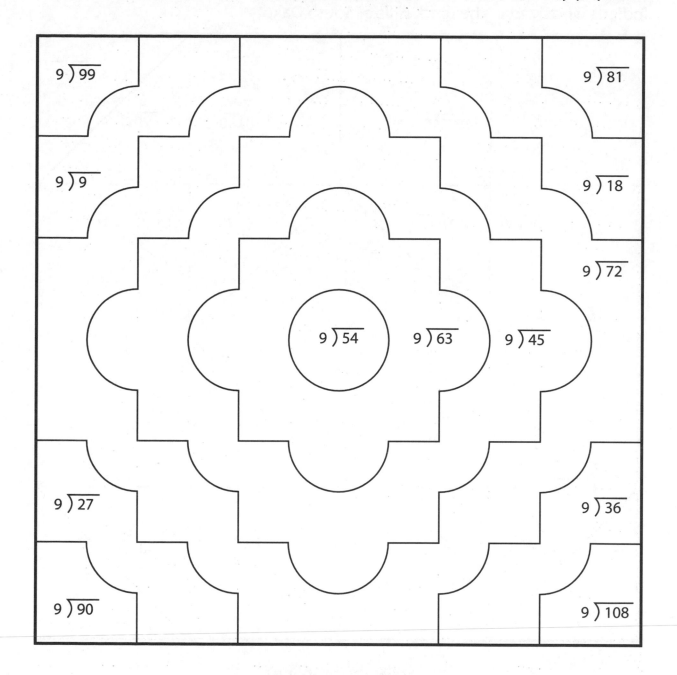

Solve the problems.

If the answer is between	Color the shape
1 and 6	yellow
7 and 12	blue

 Extra! On the back of this page, write two division problems that each have a quotient of 8.

Quilt Math   Scholastic Professional Books

Name_____

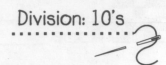

Cheyenne

Pioneers moving west probably named this quilt block after the Cheyenne Indians who lived in the Black Hills of South Dakota.

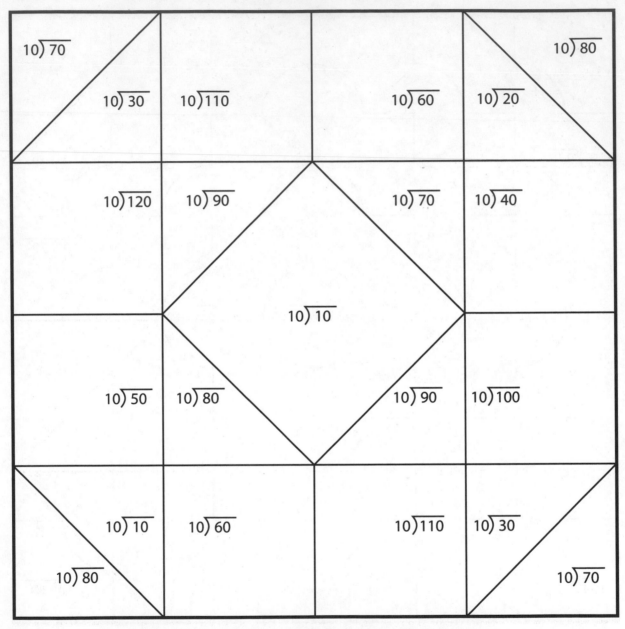

Solve the problems.

If the answer is between	Color the shape
1 and 3	orange
4 and 6	dark orange
7 and 9	black
10 and 12	yellow

Extra! On the back of this page, write two division problems that each ha~~ a divisor of 10.

98

Quilt Math   Scholastic Professional Books

Name_____

Chisholm Trail

Jesse Chisholm cut a wagon trail through the wilderness from San Antonio, Texas, to Abilene, Kansas. The trail became a popular route for cattle ranchers.

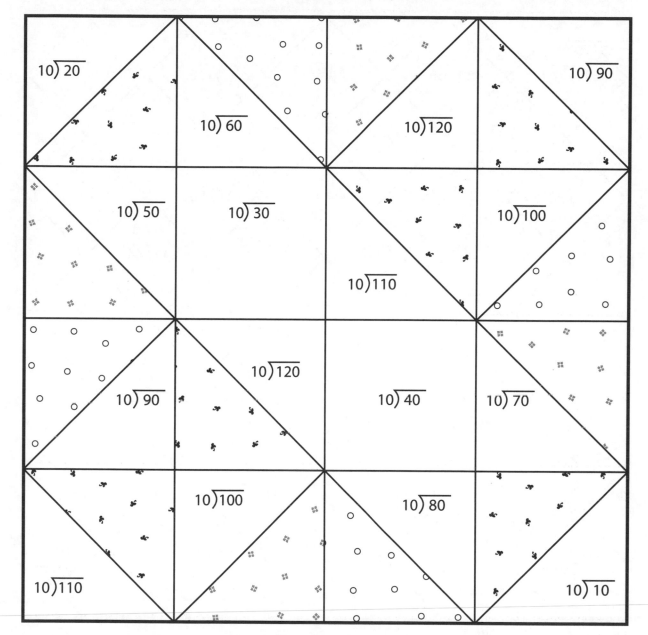

Solve the problems.

If the answer is between	Color the shape
1 and 4	orange
5 and 8	dark orange
9 and 12	green

Fill in the other shapes with colors of your choice.

Extra! The cashier has $80 in ten dollar bills. How many ten dollar bills does she have? Write the answer on the back of this page.

Quilt Math   Scholastic Professional Books

Name_____

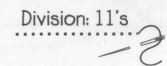

Trip Around the World

In pioneer days, this simple quilt pattern was popular for everyday quilts.

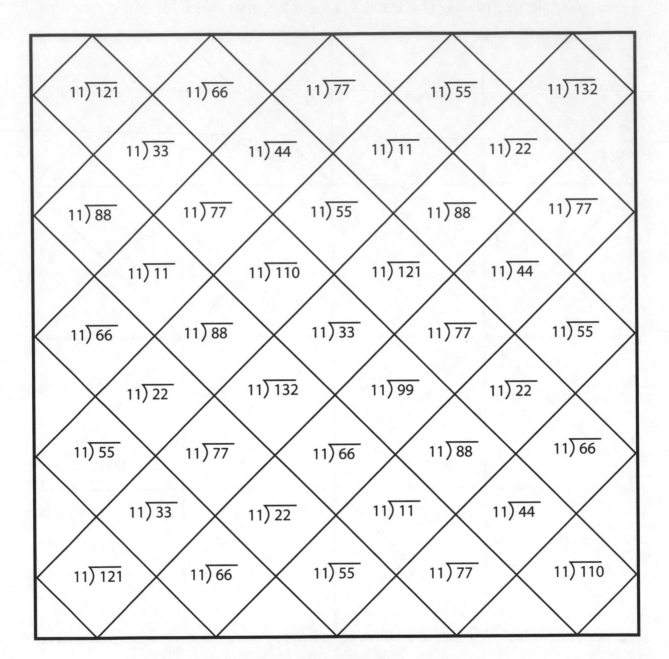

Quilt Math   Scholastic Professional Books

Solve the problems.

If the answer is between	Color the shape
1 and 4	green
5 and 8	dark orange
9 and 12	black

Fill in the other shapes with colors of your choice.

Extra! Lucy has 55 pennies. If she divides them evenly among 11 friends, how many pennies will each friend get? Write the answer on the back of...

100

Name_____

Martha Washington's Star

Martha Washington was the wife of George Washington, who was the first president of the United States.

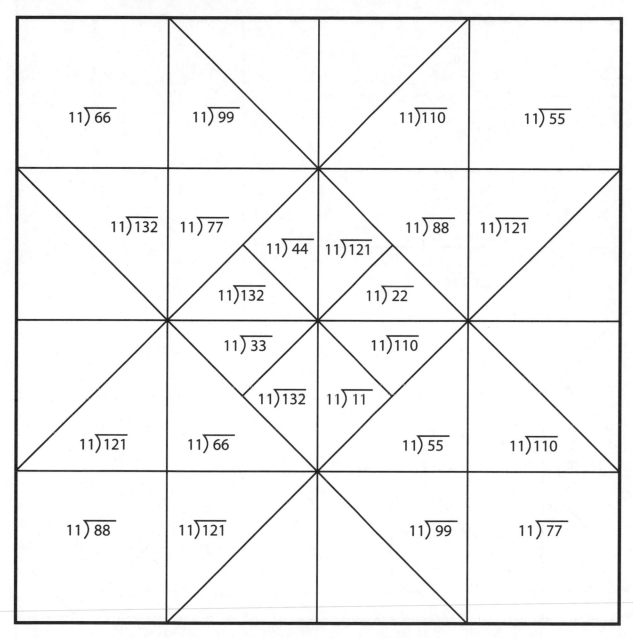

Solve the problems.

If the answer is between	Color the shape
1 and 4	yellow
5 and 8	dark orange
9 and 12	blue

Fill in the other shapes with colors of your choice.

 On the back of this page, write a division problem that has a divisor of 11 and a quotient of 5.

Quilt Math   Scholastic Professional Books

Name_____

Rail Fence

Pioneers built fences made of wooden rails to mark their boundaries and to protect their livestock.

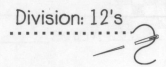

12)24

12)84

12)48

12)132

12)36   12)96   12)72   12)120

12)120   12)60   12)84   12)24

12)144

12)48

12)108

12)12

Solve the problems.

If the answer is between	Color the shape
1 and 3	light orange
4 and 6	dark orange
7 and 9	green
10 and 12	blue

 On the back of this page, write the division facts for 12 that are the most difficult for you to solve.

Quilt Math   Scholastic Professional Books

Name_____

Rolling Star

Quilt frames look like long tables with quilts stretched across the top.
People gather around all sides with needle and thread and quilt.

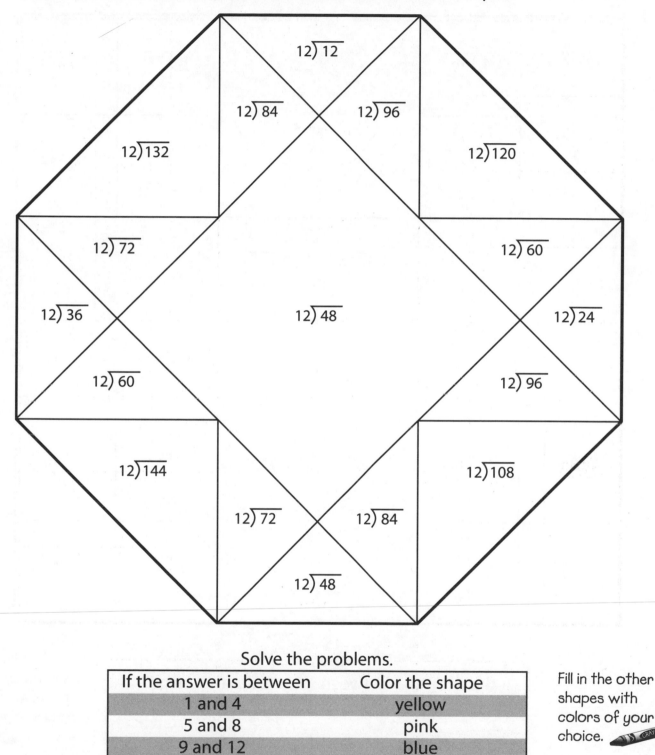

Solve the problems.

If the answer is between	Color the shape
1 and 4	yellow
5 and 8	pink
9 and 12	blue

Fill in the other
shapes with
colors of your
choice.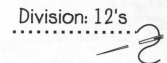

Extra! Fill in the missing numbers.

$60 \div$ ____ $= 12$ ____ $\div 1 = 12$ $120 \div$ ____ $= 12$

Quilt Math   Scholastic Professional Books

 Name_____

Covered Wagon Trail

From 1780 to 1850 thousands of Americans left their homes, friends, and families. These pioneers traveled west in covered wagons to begin new lives.

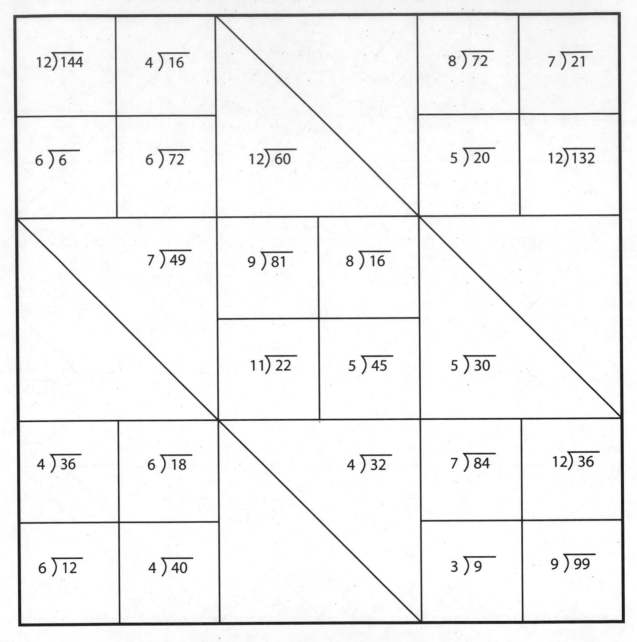

Solve the problems.

If the answer is between	Color the shape
1 and 4	green
5 and 8	dark orange
9 and 12	black

Fill in the other shapes with colors of your choice.

Extra! On the back of this page, write three different division problems that each have a dividend of 12.

Quilt Math   Scholastic Professional Books

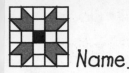

Name_____

Salt Lake City

Salt Lake City, Utah, was founded in 1847 by Brigham Young. Many pioneers stopped there to get supplies on their way to California.

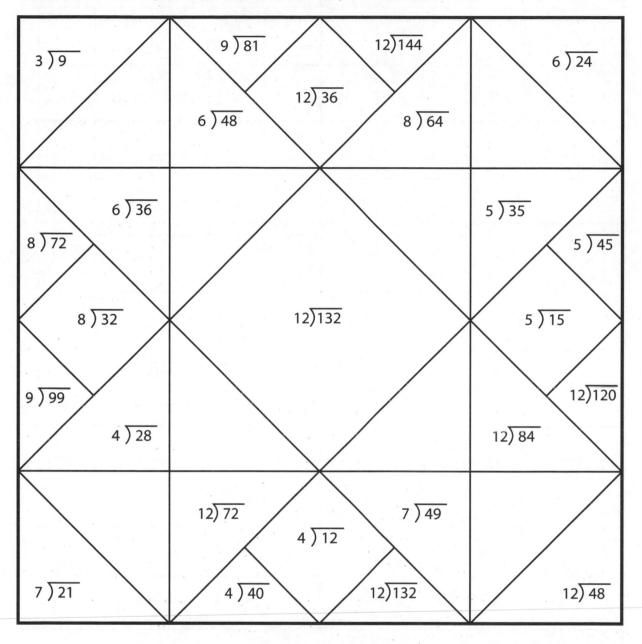

Solve the problems.

If the answer is between	Color the shape
1 and 4	green
5 and 8	dark orange
9 and 12	black

Fill in the other shapes with colors of your choice.

Extra! If you divide this number into 20, the quotient will be 1 more than that number. Write the number on the back of this page.

Quilt Math   Scholastic Professional Books

Name _____

_____
(Write the name of your quilt block here.)

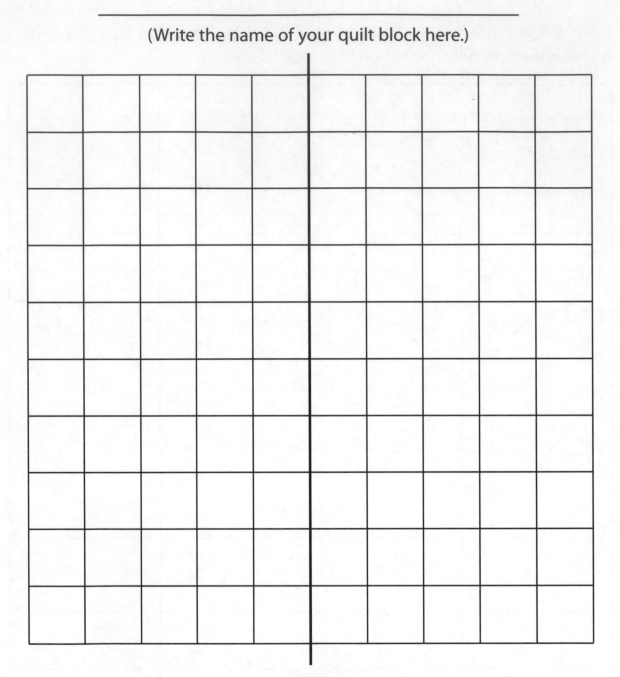

middle

Quilt Math Scholastic Professional Books

On the grid, design a quilt pattern. Each side of the pattern should be a mirror image of the other side, as you see in the examples below.

If you fold the designs in the middle, the sides will match. The two sides are called mirror images.

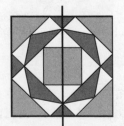

Name_____

(Use with page 108.)

1. Cut out the nine 9-box pattern blocks along the dotted lines.
2. On one pattern block, color in some of the boxes.
3. Then color the other eight blocks the same way.
4. Place the pattern blocks on the grid on page 108.
5. Slide or turn the pattern blocks on the grid to create a design.
   Look at the pictures below for ideas.

Quilt Math   Scholastic Professional Books

Name_____

(Use with page 107.)

1. On the grid below, slide or turn the pattern blocks from page 107 to create a design.
2. Glue the pattern blocks in place.

_____

(Write the name of your quilt block here.)

Quilt Math   Scholastic Professional Books

Name_____

_____

(Write the name of your quilt block here.)

On the grid, design a quilt pattern using triangles, squares, and rectangles.
Then color the shapes.

Quilt Math   Scholastic Professional Books

Name_____

_____
(Write the name of your quilt block here.)

Story quilts are made to tell a story about a time in history or family events. Make a story quilt showing something exciting that happened in your life. If you wish, on the back of the quilt block, write a story about the event you picked and describe why you chose it.

Quilt Math Scholastic Professional Books

110

Answers to the Extra! Questions

Pages 8 –10:

Answers will vary.

Page 11:

A rectangle has four sides.

▭

Page 12:

four sides

Page 13:

Answers will vary.

Page 14:

square, triangle

Page 15:

Answers will vary.

Page 16:

$24 + 24 = 48$

Pages 17 – 20:

Answers will vary.

Page 21:

6 is the missing number

Page 22:

8 sides

Pages 23 – 24:

Answers will vary.

Page 25:

168

Page 26:

436

Page 27:

Answers will vary.

Page 28:

$157 + 751 = 908$

Pages 29 – 32:

Answers will vary.

Page 33:

ten, eleven, twelve, thirteen, fourteen

Pages 34 – 39:

Answers will vary.

Page 40:

$93 - 18 = 75$

Page 41:

Answers will vary.

Page 42:

342

Pages 43 – 44:

Answers will vary.

Page 45:

four

Page 46:

Page 47:

975

Page 48:

7999

Page 49:

9753

Page 50:

odd

Page 51:

There are 108 small triangles.

Page 52:

three, four, four

Page 53:

The following numbers should be circled:

15, 16, 17, 18, 19, 20, 21, 22, 23, 24.

Pages 54 – 57:

Answers will vary.

Page 58:

The following shapes should be circled:

square, triangle, rectangle, octagon.

Page 59:

8 children

Page 60:

15 wheels

Continued

Page 61:

18 children

Page 62:

32 tires

Page 63:

4, 8, 12, 16, 20, 24, 28, 32, 36, 40, 44, 48

Page 64:

5, 10, 15, 20, 25, 30, 35, 40, 45, 50, 55, 60

Page 65:

The missing numbers are: 10, 20, 35, 55.

Page 66:

48 pretzels

Page 67:

three

Page 68:

Answers will vary.

Page 69:

7, 14, 21, 28, 35, 42, 49, 56, 63, 70, 77, 84

Page 70:

8, 16, 24, 32, 40, 48, 56, 64, 72, 80, 88, 96

Page 71:

Answers will vary. One possible answer is:
square, triangle, parallelogram.

Page 72:

9, 18, 27, 36, 45, 54, 63, 72, 81, 90, 99, 108

Page 73:

18

Pages 74 – 78:

Answers will vary.

Page 79:

The following numbers should be circled:
12, 24, 36, 48, 60, 72, 84, 96, 108, 120, 132, 144.

Pages 80 – 83:

Answers will vary.

Page 84:

4

Page 85:

Answers will vary.

Page 86:

4, 8, 12, 16, 20, 24, 28, 32, 40

Pages 87 – 88:

Answers will vary.

Page 89:

4

Page 90:

Answers will vary.

Page 91:

$6 \div 6 = 1$; $12 \div 6 = 2$; $18 \div 6 = 3$;
$24 \div 6 = 4$; $30 \div 6 = 5$; $36 \div 6 = 6$;
$42 \div 6 = 7$; $48 \div 6 = 8$; $54 \div 6 = 9$;
$60 \div 6 = 10$; $66 \div 6 = 11$; $72 \div 6 = 12$

Page 92:

Answers will vary.

Page 93:

$42 \div 7 = 6$

Page 94:

5 pieces

Pages 95 – 98:

Answers will vary.

Page 99:

8 ten dollar bills

Page 100:

5 pennies

Page 101:

$55 \div 11 = 5$

Page 102:

Answers will vary.

Page 103:

5, 12, 10

Page 104:

Answers will vary.

Page 105:

4